Never Miss a Goal Again

GET PAST *YOUR* FEAR, FAILURES,
EXCUSES, AND SELF-DOUBTS *WITH*

The Oxcart Technique
Your Blueprint for Success

TERRY L. FOSSUM

It's not the mountain that we conquer, but ourselves.
—Sir Edmund Hillary, the first person to climb Mount Everest

Never Miss A Goal Again

ISBN paperback: 979-8-9894528-3-5
ISBN hardcover: 979-8-9894528-2-8
ISBN ebook: 979-8-9894528-4-2

Printed in the United States of America, Second edition

R RAIDHO
P R E S S

SPECIAL THANKS

How do I even begin to thank all of the people who helped in the development of this book? From those experts who gave of their time and talents to contribute their sage advice, to all of those who were kind enough to read the numerous drafts and give me their honest feedback, to those who continued to encourage me along the way, from the bottom of my heart, I thank you.

Most of all, I'd like to thank my wife, Michelle, who did all of the above, and so much more. May the love we share today continue to the last days of our lives, true and timeless.

ENDORSEMENTS

Highly recommended by some of the top minds in science, business, and self-improvement in the world.

The Oxcart Technique is the most significant advancement in the science of goal setting in recent history.

–Forrest M. Mims III, named "One of the 50 best brains in science"
by Discover Magazine

I'm dedicated to helping people achieve positive, lasting behavior change, for themselves, their people, and their teams. Terry L. Fossum's book focuses on that, too. This book gives you a novel twist to the old "carrot and stick" marketing principle that is simple — and simply powerful. Whether you want a successful marriage or to become a successful teacher or to quit smoking or to just earn more money for yourself and your company — Fossum's book spotlights your way to success.

Marshall Goldsmith, named one of the Top 10 Business Minds in the World,
Author of New York Times Bestselling books Triggers,
What Got You Here Won't Get You There and The Earned Life

Whatever your dreams and goals, Terry L. Fossum's results-oriented book provides you with a truly effective version of the carrot-and-stick technique that will lift your spirits and get results.

–T. Harv Eker, Globally renown financial motivation expert,
Author, New York Times #1 Bestseller, Secrets of the Millionaire Mind

Are the old, "approved" marketing techniques not working as well as you want? To be successful in your marketing, what you need is something new, like my world-famous word-of-mouth networking technique, not something old. You see, success often results from "the uncommon application of common knowledge." And Terry L. Fossum gives you a new, uncommon application for the "common knowledge" of the 'carrot and stick' marketing principle in his book. And it works — every time!"

–Dr. Ivan Misner, NY Times Bestselling Author and Founder of
Business Network International (BNI),
the world's largest business networking and business referral organization.

Terry cuts right to the chase in identifying and overcoming every challenge in an easily relatable and clear voice. His humble candor about his own challenges and failures — and in applying the book — reinforces the great utility in this "blueprint for success" that everyone can apply for themselves.

–Paul Sean Hill, Leadership evangelist and former NASA-JSC
Director of Mission Operations

All of us, to some degree or another, are controlled by culturally ingrained myths of various sorts. As I showed how to overcome financial myths in my bestselling book, *Killing Sacred Cows*, so you, too, can overcome any kind of myth or mental barrier in your own life. How? Terry L. Fossum's new book gives you a simple but powerful technique that can help you overcome any barriers standing in your way to whatever goal you want to achieve. Check it out! It's amazingly powerful and effective!

–Garrett B. Gunderson, #1 Wall Street Journal and
New York Times Bestseller of Killing Sacred Cows

From my time as a social worker in my early career, to becoming an entrepreneur and recognized globally as an optimization expert having worked with companies like Google, Disney and Forbes, I have always counted on helping people avoid the friction of pain and move towards the joy of what motivates them. The carrot the ox enjoys and the stick he avoids in Terry L. Fossum's book will help you to be successful in everything you try. Read Fossum's book and your life will go from driving an oxcart to cruising in a Lambourgini in a flash!

–Bryan and Jeffrey Eisenberg, New York Times Bestselling Authors of Waiting for Your
Cat to Bark, Call To Action, Always Be Testing

Rooted in a scientific theory that earned the Nobel Prize in Economics in 2002, the book stands the test of scientific scrutiny. Albert Einstein said, "The definition of genius is taking the complex and making it simple." That's exactly what Terry L. Fossum has done in the book you now hold in your hands. What remains is for you to decide what you're going to do with this ticket for the rest of your life.

–Dr. Dennis Tansley, PhD, Assistant Professor, Dartmouth College; Practicing Psychologist, Veterans Administration; Major, U.S. Air Force, ret.

Terry L. Fossum's book is a testament to the genius of simplifying the complex. As a proud member of Eliances, Where Entrepreneurs Align, Terry frequently shares his wisdom with billionaires, millionaires, founders, and startups. His Oxcart Technique distills decades of research into actionable strategies that inspire and drive results. This book is not just a guide but a game-changer for anyone serious about achieving their goals. Terry's unique ability to blend science with storytelling creates a powerful resource for entrepreneurs and dreamers alike.

–David Cogan, Founder of Eliances

LEGAL DISCLAIMER

The Company, Publisher and Author disclaim any personal liability, both tangible and intangible, loss or risk incurred as a consequence of the use and application, either directly or indirectly, of any advice, information or methods presented herein.

The author has made all reasonable efforts to provide current and accurate information for the readers. The author will not be held liable for any errors or omissions that may be found. The methods contained do not guarantee success in any way. Many factors can and will alter the results you may personally experience.

The reader of this book assumes full responsibility for any action taken, and any results that occur as a result of reading and/or putting this material into effect. Readers must use their own judgment.

Many of the examples given in this book have their names and specific details altered to protect the privacy of the individuals. Any resemblance to actual events or locales or persons, living or dead, is entirely coincidental.

The author and publishers are not professional counselors, investment advisors, relationship experts, or experts in any field discussed in this book. As stated in the book, it is highly recommended that you work with experts in these fields to achieve results in these areas. Furthermore, it is recommended that you work closely with a licensed mental health professional any time you are dealing with strong emotions, as you will when enacting the methods described herein. If you are experiencing melancholy, depression, or thoughts of suicide, stop all actions, and seek qualified professional help. All information contained herein is strictly the opinion of the author, and should not be taken as direction or professional advice.

SCHEDULE TERRY TO SPEAK

Terry provides a masterful keynote speech that will entertain, inform and inspire, and get your organization into ACTION! Learn more at www.TopRatedKeynote.com.

LEARN MORE AND GET MORE

Get free stuff and more, and get on Terry's personal mailing list at www.TerryLFossum.com.

Follow Terry on Social Media everywhere!

Table of Contents

EDUCATION

APPLICATION

Wealth

Health

Relationships

FOREWORD

The definition of genius is taking the complex and making it simple.

— Albert Einstein

Now, reread Einstein's quote above.

That's exactly what Terry L. Fossum has done in the book you now hold in your hands. He's taken the complex and simplified it so anyone can benefit from putting The Oxcart Technique into practice.

Kahneman and Tversky published Prospect Theory in 1979. Prospect Theory is a theory of decision making under conditions of uncertainty or risk. This theory uses messages that are framed positively (carrots) and messages that are framed negatively (sticks) to help motivate people into action. An example of a positively framed message would be, "The more you put into yourself and your career, the more you'll get out of it!" A negatively framed message for the same situation would be, "The less you put into yourself and your career, the less you'll get out of it!"

Since 1979, message framing has been researched in a vast array of elds such as the promotion of healthy habits, communications, COVID-19 related decision making, academic and occupational decision making, economics, drug abuse, and marketing, to name a very few. The research into message framing has even been studied in neuroeconomics, which is the study of the brain's activity when people are presented with differently framed messages.

To add to this, a positively framed message, or carrot, is more likely to get people to actually do something in situations where the outcome of doing something is more certain, for example, securing a baby seat into a car, and a negatively framed message, or stick, is generally better when the outcome is more uncertain, such as career-exploration activities. But wait, there's more…

The last 30 years of research have also shown that gain-framed messages (carrots) tend to make us feel positive emotions and loss-framed messages (sticks) tend to make us feel negative emotions. This supports Terry's assertion in this book that, "Emotion, not fact, is the driver of all action." In other words, when we get a message (this book), it elicits different emotions in us, and we take action to either get rid of the negative emotion or get more of the positive emotion. Those are Negative Reinforcement and Positive Reinforcement respectively and are parts of Edward Thorndike's Operant Conditioning, which he developed in the late 1800's and published in 1905 as part of his Law of Effect.

The way Terry uses Prospect Theory in his Oxcart Technique is straightforward and easy to understand. The use of both positively and negatively framed messages tends to have the greatest impact on the greatest amount of people because we're motivated differently in different situations.

So, pay attention to what you're reading, do all of the exercises (don't just think about them, DO them), and know that this book is solidly based on decades of research. Now, take a deep breath…or two…

You don't have to remember what you just read because you can always re-read this Foreword. You could even check out the research online. My part is to show you that Terry Fossum's Oxcart Technique is solidly grounded in scientic research. Now you can read the rest of this book and practice the Technique, knowing it's the real deal.

What remains is for you to decide what you're going to do with this ticket for the rest of your life.

–Dennis P. Tansley, PhD

About Dr. Dennis P. Tansley, PhD

In his 23 years with the United States Air Force, Dr. Dennis P. Tansley, Ph.D., led teams of up to 85 subordinates and managed inventories worth up to $212,000,000 in dynamic environments during operations in the USA, Iraq, Afghanistan, Cuba, England, Turkey, Republic of Korea, Germany, Italy, and Antarctica. He's personally treated thousands of individuals, couples, and groups for a wide variety of symptoms, situations, and challenges, and led team responses to multiple suicide attempts, fatalities, and severe mishaps.

He's currently serving as a Psychologist in the Veterans Administration (VA) and as an Assistant Professor at Dartmouth College. Beyond engaging in psychotherapy with veterans, Dr. Tansley provides clinical supervision and education to Dartmouth Hitchcock Medical Center psychiatry residents and VA psychology interns/trainees. He's published and presented on an array of topics including his dissertation–Tansley, D. P., Jome, L. M., Haase, R. F., and Martens, M. P. (2007). The effects of message framing on college students' career decision-making. *Journal of Career Assessment*, 15(3), 301-316.

INTRODUCTION

"The decision to succeed does not happen once. It happens every single day; in fact, several times a day by the actions you take or do not take."

— Terry

Have you ever tried to reach a goal, but failed? You probably started with the best intentions in mind. You were "really going to do it this time!" Maybe it was a financial goal: This was your time to take it to the next level—to finally make those dreams come true, to inspire your team to success, or at least develop a nest egg that would make you comfortable in your golden years. Or maybe you were trying to get those extra pounds to come off, and stay off for good. Or perhaps you were just trying to keep or mend a relationship, to see if "happily ever after" really can come true.

But over time, the enthusiasm that was there in the beginning just seemed to wane. It wasn't that your goals weren't important anymore, but other things just seemed to get in the way. The excuses started to make sense. The fears and self-doubts crept back in. And you found yourself stuck in your comfort zone once again.

If you've ever felt that way, know this: You're not alone. In fact, according to a study from the University of Scranton, 92% of the people who set a goal fail.

92%!

And there's a reason why.

Let's take this further: Studies show that up to 90% of diets fail. And there's a reason why.

More than 50% of marriages fail at the goal of living 'happily ever after'; so much so that it's becoming a major reason the marriage rate has declined since 1970. And you guessed it: there's a reason why.

55% of salespeople consistently fail to reach their goals, 90% of network marketers fail to reach their goals, 65% of businesses fail within 10 years, over 65%

of the entire population of the United States of America fail at the goal of being prepared for retirement, and the list goes on and on.

So, why do most everyone who sets a goal fail to reach it?

Get this: Much of what we've been taught about goal setting is either incorrect, or completely wrong. That's right! The 'age-old truths' about goal setting aren't actually truths at all.

Now, I realize that's a bold statement, but the results speak for themselves!

And so do the facts.

Let's start by busting some popular myths about goal setting.

If you've studied self-improvement at all; read books on it, been to the seminars, listened to audios; pretty much anywhere, you've heard of the Harvard Goal Setting Study. The reports on this study vary, but they go anywhere from 'those who wrote down their goals made more money than all of those who didn't combined', to 'every single person who wrote down their goals achieved them.'

Countless anecdotes exist, and have been preached from stages around the world, of people who wrote down their goals, put it in a drawer, and, low and behold, years later they found that piece of paper and had achieved those goals, giving even more credence to the amazing Harvard Goal Setting Study!

Those stories are great, and many of them may even true, but the overarching truth is that those stories represent a minuscule portion of the countless people who wrote down their goals expecting them to magically come to fruition, because that's what they were told would happen and the Harvard Goal Setting Study proved it's true.

Here's the problem: The Harvard Goal Setting Study doesn't actually exist. It never happened. Harvard has confirmed it. So has Yale, and everyone else that study has been falsely attributed to. Someone completely made it up!

That's not to say that writing down your goals isn't important. It is. But just writing down your goals isn't going to do the job for you. You're going to have to work.

And that brings us to another popular belief: "All you have to do is put it out to the universe, and the universe will go to work making it happen for you." There are an overabundance books, audios, videos, trainings, and on and on and on, citing 'science' that are being gobbled up by hopeful people that are looking for an easy way to accomplish their goals.

But the truth is: There is no easy way to climb a mountain! There is no escalator to the top, no hot air balloon that you can just climb aboard that will magically lift you. It's going to take effort on your part, some hard work, and maybe a little blood, sweat, and tears!

If it was true that all you have to do is put it out there to the universe, then I would have won the lottery many times over! Now, I've never bought a ticket, but that's not what their theory says; it says I only have to put it out to the universe, not take action!

There's a saying that says "The Lord helps those who help themselves." I believe the universe acts the same way! Can you imagine if you were the universe, and people are saying "Hey, universe! Make this happen for me. I don't want to do the work, I want YOU to do the work. But I want you to give me everything I want." How would you feel?

I can only speak for myself. I'd be thinking "Look, you're acting like a spoiled child! You want something? Get up off your butt and get it yourself. I'm not going to do it for you!"

Again, I'm not saying that positive visualization, prayer, intention, and everything like it isn't important. I believe it's critical, and, quite frankly, I do it from the first moment I wake up every single morning. But by themselves they are not effective enough to get you to where you want to be, no matter what popular culture is saying.

Remember: 92% of the people who set a goal fail at reaching it. Doing what's popular or following outdated beliefs on goal setting isn't going to get you where you want to be.

So, what does work? In this book, we're going to apply actual Nobel Prize-winning science to goal setting, and give you a specific technique that, if truly applied properly, may not 100% guarantee your success (nothing will), but will, without question, <u>significantly</u> increase your odds. It will give you a specific path to run on, and the daily motivation – real motivation – to get you there.

You're going to learn how to actually harness your failure, and your eagerness to avoid it, (known in the scientific world as loss-aversion) to fuel your fire like never before.

And if these principles are applied properly to your team, your company, or your organization, their productivity will, without question, absolutely sky-rocket.

But this comes with a word of warning: If you're looking for a book that is simply written to make you feel good, and promise bunnies and unicorns with no action on your part, this isn't your book.

If you're looking for a book that will challenge your current beliefs about goal setting; perhaps even turn them completely on their ear; challenge you personally, and get you the results you're looking for, then open up your mind, get ready to work, and read on!

It won't be easy. In fact, some parts are going to be hard. But if your goals – whatever they are – are important enough to you, then it will be worth it.

Whether it's financial abundance, healthy relationships, health, or something else entirely, you truly can have it all, but you're going to have to work for it; in <u>all</u> of those areas. And you're going to have to work wisely, probably differently than you have before.

If you're ready to take that first, most important step, then take a deep breath, turn the page, and let's get started.

EDUCATION

CHAPTER 1

Passion to Move Mountains

*Passion is energy. Feel the power that comes
from focusing on what excites you.*

— Oprah Winfrey

I am often asked what I believe the single most important factor in success is.

To me, there is absolutely no doubt:

PASSION!

Without passion, it's doubtful you'll have the tenacity to see your goals to fruition. With enough passion, nearly anything is possible.

Google defines passion as, "An intense desire or enthusiasm for something." It is that enthusiasm that will make you want to spend time and energy on your goals instead of the distractions that will try to get in the way. It is that intense desire that will make you get up, dust yourself off, and continue on your path when the setbacks and disappointments try to force you to quit.

You might think that you are not a very passionate person. Maybe you didn't cry while watching Bambi, or maybe even Old Yeller didn't draw a tear. Maybe you don't exactly wake up each morning singing, "Oh, What a Beautiful Morning!" or scream at the TV when your team is losing. Or maybe you do…

Regardless, you do have passion within you. You have things that stir your emotions deeply. Things that make you angry, or happy, or driven, or frightened, or make you dig your heels in.

If you can learn to focus that passion, and harness the mighty energy that surges from it, you can break through any barrier that might otherwise hold you back!

Field Marshal Ferdinand Foch, Supreme Commander of Allied forces during World War I, once said,

"The most powerful weapon on earth is the human soul on fire."

I couldn't agree more. It's my belief that you can accomplish pretty much anything, if you're passionate enough about it. Harsh dictators have been overthrown, hopeless battles have been won, diseases have been cured, mountains conquered, lives have been saved, apparent miracles have manifested—all because of passion.

There are countless stories of people who have had astronomical setbacks, but because of their passion, they were able to overcome them, and be tremendously successful.

A 14-foot Tiger Shark bit off 13-year-old Bethany Hamilton's arm while she was surfing. Most people wouldn't consider ever again getting close to any body of water larger than a bathtub, much less continue surfing. But most people don't have Bethany's passion for surfing. Because of that passion, she dove back into the water as soon as she was able, and she is still amazingly ranked in the top 10 women surfers in the world today. The uplifting movie Soul Surfer is based on her incredible story, where she is quoted as saying, "I don't need easy, I just need possible." This mantra and her incredible courage and determination have inspired millions around the globe.

U.S. Rep. Gabrielle Giffords was shot in the head. Doctors removed nearly half of her skull to compensate for brain swelling. Most believed she wouldn't live, much less be able to speak. They didn't understand her passion for life and her steely determination. That passion is driving her to work hard every single day to speed up her recovery. It's not easy. It's extremely hard. But that doesn't stop her from trying. As difficult as it may be, she's overcoming her adversity, all of the things that might hold her back, and living life to the fullest. Today, she's speaking to crowds of thousands, hiking in the Grand Canyon, even skydiving! Her passion feeds her determination to overcome the obstacles, the fear, and the doubt and continue to improve every single day. As was said to her assailant at his hearing, "You may have put a bullet through her head, but you haven't put a dent in her spirit and her commitment to make the world a better place."

The great Swiss philosopher Henri Frederic Amiel said,

"Without passion man is a mere latent force and possibility, like the flint which awaits the shock of the iron before it can give forth its spark."

Passion is the spark that ignites the fires within us.

Passion gives us the power to turn our goals and dreams into a reality.

Passion conquers all.

You absolutely can live your dreams. You can reach your goals. Every single one of us, regardless of our background, intelligence, or gifts, can smash through any barriers that may stand in the way.

But without that passion to drive us forward, our vision blurs. Our motivation falters. Doubts conquer. Mediocrity mires us in the muck of the status quo.

Perhaps there are challenges that have held you back — seemingly insurmountable odds that make you think that there is no way you can accomplish your goals, hopes, and dreams.

My brothers and I could have believed our neighbor who said we 'would never grow up to be anything'. We could have easily said, "We have too many odds stacked against us. He's probably right. Why should we even try?"

But we chose to harness our passion and rise above the odds. Our parents taught us to learn from failure, but not to fear it, and to keep getting up, no matter how many times we were knocked down.

After getting my degree in Mechanical Engineering, I received a commission as an officer in the United States Air Force, where I was the Executive Officer for an entire group of nuclear B-52 aircraft. I was named Officer of the Year for Fairchild Air Force Base, Distinguished Graduate from Squadron Officers' School, and Humanitarian of the Year for all of Strategic Air Command.

In business, I developed a marketing force that spanned much of the globe and earned a significant amount of money doing so.

In acting and producing, I've received accolades such as winning the Best Supporting Actor and Fan Favorite at the 2021 Christian Film Festival. I've hosted shows such as Made in America.

As an author, I've reached #1 on Wall Street Journal, Amazon, and Barnes & Noble bestseller lists.

As a speaker, I've been Blessed to speak to companies, organizations, the military, and academia in different parts of the world.

I even won a survival reality show called Kicking & Screaming prime-time on Fox Network.

I'm further blessed to help build a school in Rwanda to teach marketable skills to the orphans and widows of the genocide, and funded education for families in Malawi who learn advanced farming techniques, and return to their villages after a full year to share that knowledge with others. I've been able to fund scholarships for underprivileged youth here in the United States, and much more. And I've been extremely active in the Boy Scouts of America on a local and national basis, including as a Scoutmaster for my own kids, and President of the Board of Directors for the Inland Northwest Council, BSA.

And my brothers? One of them is a successful dentist whose giving surpasses my own, and the other a former U.S. astronaut, and current head of Texas A&M University Galveston campus, who spends much of his time speaking to youth and adults alike, encouraging them to follow their dreams, and never give up. Never believe the naysayers, and learn to harness your passion.

The question is, how do you build that passion, and keep fanning its flames when the rains of resignation come pouring down?

The Oxcart Technique will empower you to cultivate the most powerful emotions you possess in your heart and soul and use them to your benefit. It will have every fiber of your being pushing you to succeed. More than that, it will spell out the actions you need to take every day to reach your goals, and continuously inspire you to reach them. It will give you an accountability system to judge your actions and monitor your success, or lack of success, each day.

Please remember: This is a WORKbook. If you are asked to stop and do visualization, or complete some quick exercises, take the time to do it. I want to help you. I want your life to be as rich and fulfilling as it can be. I want you to achieve happiness, whatever that means for you.

WHATEVER YOU DO, avoid the temptation to jump to a chapter that interests you without gaining the foundational knowledge found in the first few chapters.

Just as in learning any new skill, it is critical you understand the basic concepts of The Oxcart Technique before you can successfully apply it to your own situation.

Now it's time to harness your passion, learn how to reach your goals, and become all that you want to be. It's time to leave the past where it belongs: in your past. It's time to let loose of the things that have held you back and harness an energy you may never have known you had. It's time to build a future that you can look forward to—a future that you can be proud of!.

Let's get started!

SELF-EXAMINATION QUESTION: What is it in your own life that gets you excited? What are you passionate about?

CHAPTER 2

Banning Excuses from Your Life

He that is good for making excuses is seldom good for anything else.

— Benjamin Franklin

Let's be real: Excuses are lies we tell ourselves because we want to believe it's not our fault.

Virtually every time we've fallen short of our goal, it's because we've let excuses get in our way.

Jim Carey once starred in a movie where he couldn't tell a lie. He absolutely was not physically able to tell a lie! Although that could, and did, invite a whole host of challenges (and laughs), imagine how empowering it would be if we couldn't lie to ourselves!

Instead of saying, "I can't do that because ____(insert your own excuse)," it would sound more like, "I'm choosing not to do it because I'm letting something get in the way."

That's the truth, isn't it? In almost all cases, it's not that you can't do it, it's that you're choosing not to.

If we couldn't tell a lie, there wouldn't be any more of this:

I can't do it because...

I'm too busy right now.

I'm too tired.

I'm not smart enough.

I'm too old.

I'm too young.

I'll do it later.

These other priorities got in the way.

I don't have an education.

I'm just not like that.

Now isn't a good time.

I shouldn't have to…

Someone else should do it.

It's really their fault.

I had a troubled childhood.

I just don't have the willpower.

I need to do something else.

I'm depressed.

Something got in the way.

I don't know how.

My dog died.

My goldfish died.

Someone else's goldfish died.

I once knew a guy in my past whose goldfish died at a very young age.

The excuses people let get in the way of their success truly amaze me!

For example, people use the "I don't have time" excuse all the time. Let me see if you've heard this one:

"There's only 24 hours in a day."

Although that is true, we truly have more hours in a day available to us than we think. The difference is in how we use them.

According to a study by Provisional Living, Americans spend on the average 38 hours per week on their phone. That's over a full 24 hour day and a half on our phones every single week!

How much could you accomplish 38 hours a week, or over 5 hours a day, 7 days a week on it?

The 'I don't have time' excuse simply doesn't hold water for most of the population. If you think you don't fall into this category, plot out how you spend your time each day for a week. The truth — you have enough time to accomplish your goals. We'll find time for those things that we're passionate about.

If you focus your passion, you'll focus your time.

Listen. It's time for some tough love. You want to make a change. That's why you're reading this book. There's something you need to know:

There are two things: results or excuses.

Don't fool yourself: If it's not a result,
it's merely an excuse.

And let's face it: You're going to get a result one way or the other. It just might not be the result you're looking for.

It doesn't matter what the excuse is. It doesn't matter how real it seems to you, or how real it actually is! You CAN break through it! You HAVE TO. I guarantee you: Other people have had more stacked up against them than you do, and made it happen anyway!

My next door neighbor was hit by a drunk driver when he was out jogging. He lost the use of his legs completely. Nothing. No good. Instead of spending the rest of his life moping about what could have been and making excuses, he drives his own truck to the golf course and enjoys a good round of golf, often. He travels around the country. He plays with his grandchildren, builds things in his shop, and even walks his children's 150-pound dog! He does all of this using a wheelchair and sheer determination.

This man is an amazing inspiration to everyone!

Oprah Winfrey was sexually abused time and time again between the ages of 10 and 14. Instead of letting the weight of these atrocities crush her, she became strong enough to raise the hopes and dreams of millions around the globe.

If you're really feeling down about yourself, search the internet for "Nick Vujicic," and you'll quickly realize you have no valid excuse for anything at all. He literally has no arms and no legs, and has greatly impacted people's lives around the globe! In my opinion, he's one of the most inspirational people on the face of the planet, because he doesn't let any excuse get in his way.

So, how do you keep excuses from getting in your way?

First of all, see them for what they are: lies.

It may be true that they happened, but it's absolutely not true that they have to have any effect on you whatsoever—unless you let them.

Excuses by themselves are powerless. Only you can give them the power to keep you from reaching your goals.

Choose not to. Choose to be more powerful than your excuses. Choose to overcome them.

Adopt the belief that:

There's always a way.
It merely becomes our job to find that way.

Instead of believing that you can't do something because (insert your old excuse here), you'll believe you can do it in spite of (insert that old excuse here). You know that a way does exist to make it happen. It's merely your job to figure out what that way is. If you will stop focusing on the problem and focus on the solution instead, a solution will present itself. There's always a way!

Working through excuses can be like swimming through quicksand. They will try to hold you back, try to tire you out before you can reach your goal, try to pull you under and smother you and make you finally give up.

You simply can't let them.

And when you harness your passion to allow you to reach your full potential, they will never hold you back again.

SELF-EXAMINATION QUESTION: What people or circumstances have you let hold you back in the past? Would it have been possible, though difficult, to proceed anyway?

CHAPTER 3

Embracing Failure

*Success consists of walking from failure to
failure without loss of enthusiasm.*

— Winston Churchill

If you want to succeed, it is essential that you learn to accept, and even embrace, failure. You must learn to see it not as a foe, but as a companion to success; not as something to fear, but as a necessary piece of the puzzle that forms your life.

Let me ask you a question: What is the opposite of success? Failure, right? If you look up the antonym for 'success' in the dictionary, the answer will be 'failure'. But I'm here to tell you that it's absolutely not true. In fact, I believe the opposite it true! I believe that lack of failure is the opposite of success.

Why is that? Because not a single highly successful person in history has become successful without failing.

I talk a lot about Bill Gates, because he such a great success story. But, did you know that Bill Gates was actually a <u>failure</u>? That's right – a failure! He started a company called Traf-O-Data. Ever heard of it? No, and neither has anyone else! Well, one guy did. The guy who laughed Bill Gates and his partner Paul

Allen out of his office because the machine they were showing trying to sell him wouldn't even work!

No, I take that back. Bill Gates was absolutely not a failure. His product was a failure, but he was not. He didn't fail, because he kept going. If he would have given up on business altogether and picked up a 'Will Work For Food' sign, then maybe. But that's not what Bill did, is it?

He got up one more time than he was knocked down!

He kept on failing, until he succeeded.

Abraham Lincoln may have been one of the biggest failures in US political history! He lost his job, had a nervous breakdown, and went to war a captain and returned a lowly private! He failed nine times in politics alone! But guess what? He tried 10 times! And that 10th time made him one of the greatest presidents in the history of our country!

Was Abraham Lincoln a failure? Hardly. He could have been, but he chose not to. He chose to get up one more time than he was knocked down!

Henry Ford lost everything on five different business ventures! Vince Lombardi, one of the greatest coaches in history was told that 'he possesses minimal football knowledge and lacks motivation.'

The founder of FedEx, Fred Smith, outlined his entire business plan in a college paper, for which he received a 'C' and was told, the concept is interesting and well formed, but in order to earn better than a "C" grade, your ideas also have to be feasible.

One of the greatest basketball players of all times, Michael Jordon admits, "I've missed more than 9000 shots in my career. I've lost almost 300 games. 26 times, I've been trusted to take the game winning shot and missed. I've failed over and over and over again in my life. And that is why I succeed.

If you want to succeed, it is essential that you learn to accept, and even embrace, failure. You must learn to see it not as a foe, but as a companion to success; not as something to fear, but as a necessary piece of the puzzle that forms your life.

In fact, we are going to talk quite a bit about failure in this book, and teach you that focusing some time on the potential of failure can be enormously powerful toward helping you reach your goals!

Wait a minute! How in the world can a book on success recommend focusing on failure? If we keep talking about failure, and thinking about failure, aren't we inviting failure?

Leo F. Buscaglia, the great author, speaker, and professor, once said: "We seem to gain wisdom more readily through our failures than through our successes. We always think of failure as the antithesis of success, but it isn't. Success often lies just the other side of failure."

While we certainly don't want to spend all of our time focusing on failure, quite honestly, I believe the potential good to be gained from failure is not talked about enough!

Does an army ignore the existence of its foe? Quite the opposite. It learns everything it can about its rival. It considers any scenario in which that foe could triumph, and uses that knowledge, and incentive, to prepare for success.

Does a boxer, sports team, or politician ignore the fact that they have opposition, and that the opposition could win? No, they go to great lengths to study that possibility, and use that knowledge and that motivation to fuel their fire.

They persevere in their game plan to make sure they will triumph in battle, whatever that battle may be.

Do they dwell on defeat? Of course not. But the concern of it is always there, pushing them on.

Show me someone who hasn't failed, and I'll show you someone who has never attempted anything substantial at all.

Failure is an inevitable, though often distasteful, ingredient of success.

Have you ever tasted baking powder by itself? It tastes terrible! That may be true, but you can't bake a cake without it. It's a necessary ingredient. Failure is the same way. It's very doubtful that you can have success without failing first; in fact, most successful people have failed more times than they've succeeded!

If all we talk about is success, we're not truly preparing people for the inevitable hardships that will occur. Life isn't a fairytale. It's real. There are real challenges that have to be met head-on, and sometimes it will feel as if the only result is a really bad headache.

The question is, how do we view failure, and how do we react to it?

Do we view it as final, or temporary? Do we let the thought of it tear us down, or strengthen us?

I believe we take the word "fail" as too permanent. To me, it's a very temporary word.

In basketball, I might fail to make a basket, but that doesn't mean I'm going to stop shooting baskets! I failed at first when I was learning to walk, but that didn't stop me, no matter how many times I fell on my tookus. I failed in my first business, but I didn't fail in business. Why? I tried other businesses until I succeeded!

Whether failure becomes a permanent reality or a temporary setback is completely in your power. It will be determined by your actions, and you have complete control over them. You decide to try again, or decide to give up.

Either way, it is your response to the setback that decides your future – not the setback itself.

As Cicero, noted Roman author, orator, and politician said around 50 BC (also Grover on Sesame Street in 1969),

"Where there is life, there is hope."

So, understanding that every single person who has succeeded at anything noteworthy has failed and failed and failed, if you're not failing, you should be worried! That probably means that you're not pushing your boundaries; maybe not heading toward success very quickly, or perhaps not even at all! On the other hand, if you're failing, I want you to stand up and cheer, "Yes! I'm failing! I must be on the path to success!"

Never forget: As long as you are alive, you still have power over your life and its outcome.

You have the power to succeed. It's been given to you by someone much more powerful than you, and much more powerful than the odds stacked against you. Call on that power, reset your path, and resume your journey to victory.

FAILURE

Failure is not something to cower from or fear.
Failure is not some great giant that can overpower
you and take away your will to fight.

You will stand up strong in the face of failure and scream
with all of your courage and might: "You may have seized
the moment, but you will not seize the day. As long as there
is breath in my lungs and blood in my veins, I have been
given the power to succeed, and succeed I will. You cannot
conquer my hope. You cannot smother my dreams.

I accept and take responsibility for my actions or inactions
that gave you power temporarily. Now I take back that
power because it's mine to wield, and no one else's.

I know you will follow me on my journey to success, tempting
me to stumble, and hoping that I do. But if I fall, I will
get up and press on. If I rest, it will only be to gain my
strength for the next mountain I must climb. And if I look
back to see you, it will only be to give me the steel of will
to press on, no matter the obstacles you put in my way.

I see you, and I rebuke you. Now, get behind me, so
I may see my way, once again, to victory."

SELF-EXAMINATION QUESTIONS: What are some times you have failed in the past? How did you react to them? How will you react to failure from now on?

CHAPTER 4

Comfort Zone

"A ship is always safe at shore. But that's not what it is made for."

— Albert Einstein

If we were to boil down the single biggest reason most people don't reach their goals, it would be this: they keep reverting back to their comfort zone.

The overwhelming amount of people know what they're supposed to do to reach their goals. They know the actions they're supposed to take. Odds are, they've been trained on them, or can certainly learn how through advanced studies, or even searching the internet!

That's not the problem. The problem is actually TAKING THOSE ACTIONS on a consistent basis.

Instead of taking the steps to reach our goals which lie outside the comfort zone, we waste our time doing the things that are comfortable, but don't actually take us toward our goal. In fact, those actions actually take us away from our goal, because another hour, another day, another week goes by, and, over time, the self-doubts creep in, the excuses start to seem real, and the fear of failing – again – begins to paralyze us.

The comfort zone is where people and dreams go to die, and yet that's where most people live their lives.

I equate the comfort zone to hyperthermia. I've had many adventures in the wilderness all around the world, and an interesting thing about hypothermia is at first you feel cold, so your body tries to do something about it. It shivers, and that shivering is your body's reaction trying to generate heat. You'll continue shivering for awhile, but at some point, it gives up. It stops fighting back, and then you don't shiver anymore. And you don't even feel cold anymore. You just go numb, and, eventually, you fall asleep, and you die.

It's the same thing with your comfort zone, isn't it? The more you stay in your comfort zone, the more comfortable you feel. To begin with, maybe you start trying to fight back. You start shivering metaphorically.

You start trying to produce some action, but maybe that action doesn't work at first. So you try it again. You shiver a little more, and then it doesn't work. And then, eventually, you give up, And you feel numb in your own sort of way, and you fall asleep in your own sort of way, and then you die in your own sort of way. The comfort zone is where people and dreams go to die.

In order to reach ANY significant goal, you're going to have to get uncomfortable! You most likely heard "If you continue to do what you've always done, you'll continue to get what you've always got", and it's absolutely true. If you WANT different, you have to DO different! And 'different', almost by definition, is uncomfortable; in most cases, that's why you haven't done it!

You've continued to do what you've always done because it's comfortable. Whether it's in your business, in sales, your relationships, your health – ANY goal – in order to further that goal, you're going to have to get out of your comfort zone!

Here's the problem: Most of the self-improvement that's being taught today actually keeps people IN their comfort zone!

Current popular mantras like "dream it and it will come", "Put it out to the universe, and the universe will make it happen" and "All you have to do is manifest it, and miracles will occur" make people FEEL great! "Wow! All I have to do is think 'happy thoughts', and I'll reach my goals!"

BULL.

I'm sorry if I'm hurting anyone's feelings, but it just isn't true!

The University of Scranton study showed us that 92% of the people who set goals fail. And these are people who are following the conventional wisdom taught today.

But wait a minute – isn't positive visualization important? Absolutely. It is an important piece of the puzzle. But it's only a piece of the puzzle, and there's been a missing piece for far too long.

What is that missing piece of the puzzle?

To begin the discussion, let's look at actual science. Nobel Prize-winning science. In 1979, Kahneman and Tversky won the Nobel Prize when they applied Prospect Theory to Economics. Prospect Theory taught us, in simplified terms, that overall we'll do more to avoid pain than go toward pleasure. Again, we'll do more to avoid pain than to go toward pleasure. So, in economics, we tend more toward taking actions that avoid loss than achieve gain. In other words, we don't want to lose money more than we want to gain money.

But what if we applied that concept to goal setting; the concept that we'll do more to avoid pain than to go toward pleasure?

We associate getting out of our comfort zone with pain. It's uncomfortable, and we don't like it. It's something we want to avoid! And that's why we'll do other, more comfortable things that don't take us toward our goal. If you've ever said "I just didn't have time to get to that", odds are that you really did! You just wasted time on things that were more comfortable! If you find yourself procrastinating, it's because you want to remain comfortable! If you find the self-doubts and fears creeping in and keeping us from moving forward, it's the exact same concept: they're uncomfortable and we want to avoid them! So we stay in our comfort zone, and our goals evade us once again.

And because we'll do more to avoid pain that go toward pleasure, the pleasure of positive visualization isn't powerful enough to keep us out of our comfort zone! That's the most important thing to recognize. Again, positive visualization is very important, but it's simply not enough to keep us out of our comfort zone on its own.

Sure, if we go to some exciting conference, or read a motivational book, or listen to an inspirational podcast, it might get us into action for a little while. But before long, the excuses, self-doubts, fears, and everything else we experience outside of our comfort zone begin to overwhelm us, and over time we find ourselves back into the same, comfortable habits that kept us from reaching our goals before.

The same concept applies to marriages. During the 'honeymoon stage', everything is great! But then reality and the often uncomfortable nature of it begins to creep in; and that's where the real work begins. The average person only lasts a few weeks on a diet before the old bad habits begin to creep back in, and an estimated 90% of gym goers quit after only 3 months.

So what's the answer? Well, if we'll do more to avoid pain that we will to go toward pleasure, then we need to create enough pain to kick us out of our comfort zone!

Everyone is focused on the 'why', as in 'why I WANT to reach my goal'. That's still important; but even more important is 'why I MUST reach my goal.' What kind of a scenario can I create in my mind where failure is absolutely not an option; where I'll do whatever it takes to keep from failing at this – including stick to the daily actions that will take you toward your goal, no matter what.

Tony, a gentleman who I was recently working with, told me the story of going for his CDL, or Commercial Driver's License. Understand, this was a very difficult task for Tony. He has a challenge with testing, and has to work harder than many others do. Add to this that he has trouble staying on track, and as he admitted, is always avoiding the hard tasks. It wasn't the carrot, or positive visualization, of driving a garbage truck that kept Adam on task. It was the fact that if he didn't pass, he had no way to support his wife and two special needs children. This feeling of pain was greater than the pain of getting out of his comfort zone, studying his butt off, and taking a test that he was incredibly uncomfortable taking. The result? He passed, and now has a very good job, complete with benefits. Even more so, the boost of confidence he got from that success has him studying for an associate's degree so he can qualify for an even better job and, in his words, setting a great example for his sons and setting a legacy for his family.

Now he's implementing this concept every single day to stick to his next goal, and every single goal he has for the rest of his life.

It's time for you to learn exactly how to do it yourself, and it all begins with a parable.

SELF-EXAMINATION QUESTION: Why haven't you taken the actions List out the fears and self-doubts that have kept you in your comfort zone in the past.

CHAPTER 5

The Oxcart Parable

Happiness is not ready made. It comes from your own actions.

— Dalai Lama XIV

Telling stories has always been the single most effective teaching method known to man. It started when the first cavemen would act out scenarios and paint pictures on walls, and continues with the best trainers and presenters in the world today. We all learn best from stories/pictures.

The following is adapted from an old classic, modified to teach the lessons we'll cover in this book. Read it closely, though, as we'll be referring back to it many times in the upcoming pages.

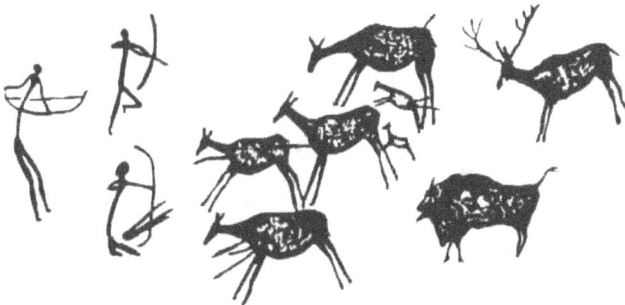

THE FARMER AND THE OXCART

There was once a farmer who lived on very fertile land, but had no way to get his crops to the market just across the river.

"Why don't you build a bridge?" the village elder asked him.

"I'm a farmer!" he replied. "I don't know how to build a bridge!"

"Ask the carpenter," the elder suggested. "He knows how to build many things."

And, sure enough, the farmer learned from the carpenter how to build a bridge, and got to work building it.

Now the farmer had his bridge, but he had no way to pull his cart full of vegetables across the bridge to the market, so he bought an ox from the village elder. It was a good ox, a strong ox, but when he brought it home and attached it to his cart, it refused to pull the cart anywhere!

"This ox is no good," he said to the elder. "I want my money back!"

"How did you motivate him?" the elder asked.

"Motivate him? He's an ox! He should know what to do and do it."

"Do you always do what you're supposed to, or do you need to be motivated sometimes? Find out what he likes, and reward him when he does right."

The farmer knew the ox's favorite treat was carrots, sweet and juicy, so he dangled a carrot just in front of the animal's head, and the ox moved forward to get it, pulling the cart behind him. Every once in a while the farmer let the ox catch the carrot so he wouldn't get discouraged.

This worked great, as long as the ox was hungry. But when he wasn't, it didn't work at all!

Angry again, the farmer approached the elder. "What am I supposed to do when the carrot doesn't do the trick? Sit beside the road until he's hungry enough? That just won't do!"

"What do you do when you don't feel like working, but know you have to anyway?"

"I think of how the crops will rot in the field, and my family will starve. That gets me out of bed no matter how tired I am!"

"So, what is it that the ox doesn't like?"

"He hates for anything to touch his tail. My son made the mistake of grabbing it one day, and nearly paid the price!"

"At the times when the carrot doesn't work, try tapping his tail with a stick."

That worked so well that most times just showing the ox the stick was enough to get him going.

The farmer was sure proud of the shrewd purchase he had made. "That's the best ox I've ever had!"

Sometimes the carrot worked, sometimes the stick worked, but using them both together, he always got his crops to market.

SELF-EXAMINATION QUESTION: What does the parable mean to you? What is represented by the carrot? The stick? The bridge? The market? The village elder? The crops rotting in the fields? The farmer let the ox get the carrot everyone once in a while; what does that represent? How does this parable relate to you reaching your goals?

CHAPTER 6

Introduction to The Oxcart Technique

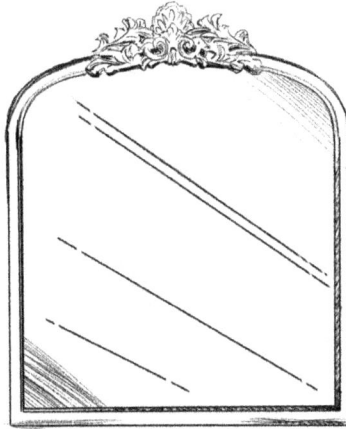

*I am not a product of my circumstances. I
am a product of my decisions.*

— **Stephen Covey**

In the Forward of this book, Dr. Dennis Tansley quoted Albert Einstein as saying "The definition of genius is taking the complex and making it simple" and graciously related this to the Oxcart Technique by saying "That's exactly what Terry L. Fossum has done in the book you now hold in your hands."

This is the point where we take the Nobel Prize-winning science of Prospect Theory that Dr. Tansley did his PhD dissertation on, combine it with the Elaboration Likelihood Model developed by Petty and Cacioppo, and add in a generous dose of hard-earned street smarts, years of failure and success, and more than a dash of common sense, and reveal that missing piece of the puzzle that makes all the difference in the world from the 92% of the people who fail at reaching their goals, and... you.

You're going to learn how to use the most powerful weapon in your arsenal. The weapon the 'feel-gooders' don't like to talk about, but actually will propel you to success much more quickly and effectively than any other tool.

What is this tool? This missing piece of the puzzle? You've probably figured it out already: The stick.

We're going to teach you to wield this weapon, this tool, in such a way that it doesn't tear you down; quite the opposite. You'll use the stick to build a fire inside of you, a fire that builds that passion to blow past your fears, your self-doubts, and your excuses; and propel you out of your comfort zone.

And even more importantly, it will continue to do so day after day after day, until you finally reach that goal you've been striving for; and even after that to make sure you don't backslide from there.

That being said, remember: this technique is not for everyone! If you're someone who is looking for the easy fix or simply to feel good, or who allows themselves to get dragged down in the face of challenge, this may not be for you! You are going to be facing some very real, very deep emotions implementing this technique! But if you're someone who is tired of holding yourself back, and ready to fight for yourself and your future, then here we go.

Let's start by digging into the Farmer and the Oxcart parable.

The farmer in the parable identified three major factors that led to his ultimate success:

- **The carrot:** that thing that was so enticing for the ox that it made him want to move toward it.
- **The stick:** that thing the ox moved away from to avoid.
- **The bridge:** the plan to get where he wanted to go.

These are the exact steps that you're going to take.

The carrot and the stick are the motivating factors, both good and bad, that will, if used correctly, provide you with both the ongoing inspiration and the kick in the butt you'll need to keep moving toward your goal when times get tough or complacency sets in.

I am not a product of my circumstances. I
am a product of my decisions.
—Stephen Covey

Your "carrot" is going to be called your Success Scenario. This is a description of how good that aspect of your life is going to look when you achieve your goal, be it weight loss, higher income, better relationships, or whatever appeals to you.

Your "stick" is called your Failure Scenario, or what that aspect of your life will look like if you don't achieve your goal. For example, what will your life look like if you don't lose that weight, or set up a retirement fund?

Your "bridge" is your Action Plan, the exact steps you'll need to take on a daily basis to make sure you achieve your Success Scenario and avoid your Failure Scenario.

Therefore, the three main components of The Oxcart Technique are:

- A Success Scenario (the carrot)
- A Failure Scenario (the stick)
- An Action Plan (the bridge)

To begin your mastering of this technique, let's apply it to an area that's near and dear to many people's hearts: football.

In Texas, football isn't just a game — it's a way of life. But a high school football coach was pulling out his last remaining hair trying to motivate his team to do their best at the daily practices. They were going through the motions, but just seemed to have lost their passion. Worst of all, it was showing in their performance. The team was looking at their first losing season in over 20 years.

One day before practice, the coach called the team into the locker room. "Today, we're going to start with something a little different," he barked. "We're going to do a little visualization."

The groans ensued. "Aw, c'mon, Coach! Can't we just get on the field and practice?"

"Oh, we will," the coach agreed. "But before we do, I want you guys to tell me what it would feel like to win the homecoming game against our rivals."

"Well, it would feel great, Coach," one of the players quipped.

"I know that, but why would it feel great? Give me more detail."

"Well, Coach," a lineman offered, "the last time we played them, those jerks were talking some serious trash. It would be great to make them eat their words."

"Sure," another player agreed, "and there's nothing like going to school the next day wearing our jerseys after a big homecoming win. We're the heroes of the school!" You could feel the excitement starting to build.

"Yeah, there's that," the quarterback, Tom, countered. "And there's the homecoming dance that night! Talk about a riot! Everybody congratulating us, giving us high fives — it'll be awesome!"

"No doubt!" another added. "And the roar of the crowd as they're counting down the final seconds of the game —that's the most exciting thing in the world!"

"Ok, guys," the coach's voice boomed.

So if I'm hearing you right, you would consider a Success Scenario something like:

It's near the end of the homecoming game, and you are winning. The crowd is on their feet as they're screaming at the top of their lungs, counting down the final seconds of the game. As the scoreboard hits zero, your winning score flashes, and the stadium erupts into pandemonium. The homecoming dance is one you'll remember forever, as everyone takes notice when you walk in the room, crowding around you and telling you how awesome you played. Then, the next day at school, wearing your jerseys and walking through the rows of about five million high fives to your classes, you'll feel like you're on top of the world."

"Does that sound about right?"

"Heck, yeah! That's it! And it sounds awesome!"

"And how do you all feel right now?" the coach asked. The chorus of replies rang out:

"Epic!"

"Awesome!"

"Like I could fly!"

"Like Amy Johnson will finally notice I'm alive!" A sea of laughs, taunts, and jeers met the last comment.

"And what are you willing to do to make those feelings a reality?" the coach challenged.

"Because to tell you the truth, it's not looking good. What you're doing so far isn't going to get you anywhere near as far as you want to go."

About half of the team, led by Tom, the quarterback, jumped in. "Whatever it takes!

I want to hear the cheers of the crowd, and feel the pride of going to that dance and walking the halls of the school with my head held high. So we need to step it way up!

I want to actually live that Success Scenario thing Coach is talking about! And it's worth working a lot harder for!"

This group was obviously highly motivated by the carrot, or the prospect of gain: What it would feel like if they won.

The other half of the team, led by the lineman, Jake, disagreed. "C'mon, Coach! We're already doing everything we can! We're out here every day, busting our butts. We just need to catch a break, that's all!"

Visualizing the "carrot," or the Success Scenario, wasn't enough to drive them harder than they already were trying.

Knowing he only had about half of the team on board, the clever coach continued. "Ok, here's another question for you: How would you feel if we lost the mighty Homecoming Game —and they kicked our butts?"

"Dude! That would suck! BIG TIME!" Big Jake, their star lineman, shouted. "Having to see that jerk's face in my mind, talking trash like he did last year, grinning that stupid grin 'cause he was better than me on the field! No way I'm going to live with that!"

"He's right," another added. "Can you imagine watching their whole team celebrating after the countdown clock hits zero, and the look on our fans' faces when we lose?

That would be TOTALLY terrible!"

"Not nearly as bad as going to the dance afterward, and school the next day. I don't even want to think about that," said another lineman who was standing near Big Jake.

"Yeah, I hate it when they come up to you with that pitying look on their face and say, 'That's okay, Kevin. You gave it your best shot.' That drives me insane!"

"So, you're telling me that a Failure Scenario," the coach summarized, "would be something like:

The Homecoming Game just ended, and we lost. The other team is celebrating on the field, and our fans are slowly shuffling out of the stadium, silent and gloomy. The dance has a different feel to it, and the next day at school is filled with half-baked pity. The front page of the newspaper talks about how our rivals wiped the field with our jerseys. Our toughest lineman, Jake, has recurring nightmares about that jerk making fun of him, and Amy Johnson will end up marrying that stupid captain of the debate team instead of our own great teammate.

"Is that about right?" ended the coach.

"No, that's NOT about right," growled Big Jake, like he was about to smash something.

"Since you put it that way, Coach, there's no way in the world I'm going to allow that to happen. That would just suck too badly." His comments were met with loud, angry agreement by his group of friends.

He continued, "I couldn't bear knowing that guy was out there talking about how he beat me. It ain't gonna happen!" He pounded his helmet against the wall. "Look, guys, I don't care if we have to spend eight hours a day out here from now until game day — I'm not gonna let down our team and our school. Coach is right. And I hate to say it, but our quarterback is right, too. We need to do more — a heckuva lot more!"

The stick, or the fear of loss, was a much bigger motivator for Jake and his buddies than the prospect of gain.

"Okay, gents," the coach responded, "it looks like we all agree that we need to do more.

But what does that mean?"

It was time to set up the actual Action Plan itself. The newly inspired team started brainstorming ideas.

"Okay — conditioning before school. We all have to be there. No excuses!"

"Yeah, and at lunch, we need to quiz each other on plays."

"And we need to watch what we eat better. Cut down on the junk. We need every edge we can get!"

"Are you kidding? I need my junk food," a player retorted. "It's what I do!"

"Look, fool, are you willing to risk living that Failure Scenario Coach talked about so you can have a little junk food?" asked the lineman. "Is it really worth it?"

"I guess not. The sight of seeing five million high fives down the hallway is a lot stronger than my gut bombs! For me, junk food is OUT!"

"Now you're talking! And at practice," Tom said, "all of us need to give absolutely everything we've got! No more goofing around for half the time we're out there! At the end, we need to crawl back to the locker room because we used up all our energy on the field. All in or nothing at all!"

"That's right! All in or nothing at all!" yelled Jake. "Let's hear it, everybody — at the top of your lungs — 'All in or nothin' at all!'"

"That's right! All in or nothin' at all!" yelled the quarterback. "Let's hear it everybody!

At the top of your lungs! 'ALL IN OR NOTHING AT ALL!'" "ALL IN OR NOTHIN' AT ALL!"

"ALL IN OR NOTHIN' AT ALL!"

"ALL IN OR NOTHIN' AT ALL!"

Arms pumping in the air and slapping each other on their helmets, or on their shoulder pads, back pads, and front pads, the entire team ran out of the locker room, putting their helmets on as they ran, with grim and gritty looks on their faces.

'How about THAT! What have I unleashed?!' the coach smirked to himself as he clutched his clipboard and ran out after them, trying to catch up and get in front. 'Just what I wanted!'

To keep the entire team fired up each and every day — both those who were motivated by the Success Scenario and those who were motivated by the Failure Scenario — the coach posted both scenarios, along with their Action Plan of daily activities, on the cork board in the locker room and taped them on the walls and lockers of the locker room. Then, to create the constant reminder that would keep them motivated for the long run, he had a different teammate read it out loud — and LOUDLY, with GUSTO — to the entire team before morning and afternoon practice. Every day, he had them visualize both scenarios and rededicate themselves, enthusiastically — with lots of shouting and backslapping — to the daily actions on their plan.

Needless to say, it was an overwhelming victory — 35-3! Jake was everywhere on defense, with 14 unassisted tackles and 9 assisted tackles. And the quarterback, Tom, had a fantastic night, too, with two touchdown passes and his own touchdown run from the 28 yard line. The crowd screamed and shouted themselves hoarse as the game clock counted down, revelry ensued, the dance was a smash hit, and about ten million High Fives were given the next day at school.

(But Amy Johnson still dated the Captain of the Debate Team — you see, he, too, used The Oxcart Technique, and won the State Debate Championship. Hey! Competition is tough out there!) Now that you've heard the quick synopsis, it's time to learn the important details of the steps you will use to climb your way to the top.

All in, or nothing at all — right? ALL IN OR NOTHING AT ALL!!!

SELF-EXAMINATION QUESTION: If you were on that football team, which would be more likely to get YOU into action: The Success Scenario, The Failure Scenario, or a bit of both?

CHAPTER 7

Daily Declaration

*People often say that motivation doesn't last. Well, neither
does bathing. That's why we recommend it daily.*

— Zig Ziglar

Please read this carefully: The step you are learning right now is the single most
important step in the entire book.

Make no mistake: If you do this step, your odds of reaching your goals are
greatly increased. If you choose not to, your chances are slashed.

It's a simple, but exceedingly powerful step that will only take about three minutes out of your day, and give you amazing results.

What is this critical step in helping you achieve your goals?

In the story in the previous chapter, the coach had the players establish three
things:

- A Success Scenario (the carrot)
- A Failure Scenario (the stick)
- An Action Plan (the enhanced workouts)

He then had the players post all three in the locker room and read them out
loud twice a day.

This is exactly what you want to do as well.

To begin with, write your Failure Scenario, your Action Plan, and your Success Scenario, each on separate pieces of paper.

You'll gain much more detail on exactly how to do each of these as you read further in this chapter and the rest of the book.

At the bottom of your Action Plan, put an arrow going to the left and to the right, as shown below.

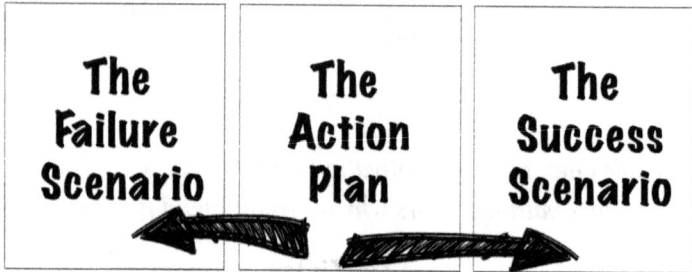

The arrows show that if you perform the tasks on your Action Plan each day, it will take you toward your Success Scenario. If you don't perform the tasks on your Action Plan that day, you'll edge toward your Failure Scenario.

After you've written down all three pages, post them where you will see them every day, with your Failure Scenario on the far left, your Action Plan in the middle, and your Success Scenario on the far right, as you see above.

You can think of it like a movie that has two alternate endings. If the hero does the right things, he succeeds in his quest and saves the world. That's the Success Scenario.

If he doesn't do what he needs to do each day, he fails, and the world ends. That's the Failure Scenario.

The Action Plan outlines the actions he'll take every day that determine his ultimate success or failure.

Only in this case, you're the hero, and this is your real life.

Either scenario could end up being your reality.

The great news is, you have complete control over which ending ultimately occurs, and you've identified those daily actions that will determine your ultimate success or failure.

Again, it is absolutely critical that you post these pages where you'll see them every single day, and read them out loud twice a day, every day.

First you'll read the Failure Scenario, then the Action Plan, and finally the Success Scenario.

Why is this absolutely critical?

> *The decision to succeed does not happen once.*
> *It happens every single day.*
> *In fact, it happens multiple times a day by*
> *the actions we take, or do not take.*

We've all heard we have greatness within us. We've all heard that whether we think we can or whether we think we can't, we're right. I believe these things are absolutely true. Yet we've tried to reach different goals, and sometimes we've been successful. Sometimes we haven't.

All too often we start out with great intentions, but the motivation seems to fade away over time, and we often find we didn't make much headway over the long run.

If we push a ball to start it rolling, we can only expect that at some point it will begin to slow down, and eventually stop. To keep it rolling, we need to push it again, and again, and again.

Yet, all too often we expect something different when we set goals. We set the goal once, and we expect to keep that same enthusiasm over the long run.

We won't.

It is critical to keep both our Success and Failure Scenarios in front of our faces, motivating us constantly.

If that farmer puts away the carrot or the stick, the ox will stop moving. It's amazing how quickly our memory, and our passion, fades.

Why is this? We act on the predominant force that is driving us at the moment. Simply put, whatever is in front of our face gets our attention, and our action. If a tasty box of Girl Scout cookies is staring us in the face, we want to act on it, right now (especially the Thin Mints, or the Samoas — okay, or any of them). If those cute shoes, or a new power tool, or both, are calling our name, we may be forced to purchase them. If that hot new coworker is hitting on us at the office party — well, you get the idea. Whatever is in front of us at the time draws our attention and tempts us to act on it. Only by keeping our long-term goals, dreams, and aspirations directly in front of our face can we have any hope of achieving them.

This is why it's critical to have all of the pages of your Oxcart Technique where you can see them, and why it's critical to read them, out loud, at least twice per day, in the appropriate order: first the Failure Scenario, followed by your Action Plan, and finally your Success Scenario. Otherwise, life gets in the way, and the demands of our daily schedules cloud our long-term dreams and aspirations. Time wasters like television or online browsing suck the hours out of our days that we could use toward developing better relationships, or building retirement income, or whatever your goal may be.

In fact, this is exactly why Dr. Bill Toth, author, father, and speaker with an emphasis on neuroscience, recommends taping them directly on your television and computer!

If you read your Scenarios out loud twice a day, every day, they will become a powerful ally in reaching your goal. They'll make you yearn to take the actions on your Action Plan, and will help inspire you to do so every single day.

SELF-EXAMINATION QUESTION: Are you truly committed to reaching your goal? Is it important enough to you to post your 3 pages, and read them out loud every morning and every night to keep you focused on accomplishing your Daily Action Plan every single day?

CHAPTER 8

Emotion Is the Driver of All Action: Developing Your Success and Failure Scenarios

Either you run the day, or the day runs you.

— Jim Rohn

The Success and Failure Scenarios are a critical part of The Oxcart Technique.

Why? Again, we're motivated by two very different things: the strong emotions caused by the prospect of a gain that is very important to us or the roaring emotions caused by the fear of loss of something critically important to us.

Think back to the parable about the farmer at the beginning of this book. The farmer can do two things to motivate the ox to walk forward and pull the cart: dangle a carrot in front of his face, so as he walks forward to try to get the carrot he pulls the cart, or touch the ox's tail with a stick. The ox tries to walk away from the uncomfortable feeling of the stick, thereby pulling the cart. Different things might work differently at different times, but both are forms of motivation.

It was the same thing with the football team story in Chapter 5. Half of them were motivated by the Success Scenario of all the cheering and the high fives. The other half were more motivated by the fear of loss, or their Failure Scenario. There was no way they were going to let that happen!

It's the same concept here.

Whatever your goal or aspiration, you are going to be drawn by the prospect of gain, moving toward the potential reality of the Success Scenario, and away from the fear of loss described in the Failure Scenario.

Have you noticed that many of the commercials on TV first show someone who's having a terrible time because they lack a certain product, and then show how great that person's life is now that they have their product? It's the same thing:

They start by showing you the stick: "Do you see how miserable this person is without our product? You don't want to be like them." Then they dangle the carrot: "Do you see how much happier they are with our product? If you buy our product, you can be that happy, too!"

Why do they use this method? Because it works! Always! You've used this method many times yourself. With your kids: "If you don't do this, you'll get punished, but if you do, you'll get a reward;" with subordinates: "If you do your work well, you might get a raise. If you don't, you might get fired;" with your spouse — well, you get the idea!

At different times, and for different situations, either the carrot (the Success Scenario) or the stick (the Failure Scenario) could be a more powerful motivating force for you.

For instance, if your much-desired goal is to earn enough extra money to go on a cruise, there may not be an extremely negative driving force. The worst that could happen is you'll experience some disappointment by not being able to go on this much-wanted vacation.

The prospect of gain, on the other hand, may be your major driving force. The vision in your Success Scenario of you sitting by the pool on the cruise ship, sailing off to some tropical location, sipping something with a tiny umbrella in it, feeling completely pampered, may be the force that drives you the most in this example.

In other circumstances, the stick, or Failure Scenario, may be more powerful. I love Brad Pitt's quote in the movie Moneyball:

"I hate losing even more than I want to win, and there's a difference."

Let's take finances as an example. You may not be very motivated by having a big house or a luxury car. But on the other hand, being poor in your retirement years and not being able to afford food or medication for you or your spouse may scare the heck out of you. In this case, your Failure Scenario may actually drive you harder than your Success Scenario.

Again, this is the power of harnessing both the pain of potential failure and the pleasure of success to inspire you to take the actions you need to take to reach whatever goals are truly important to you.

For this exercise to be as effective as possible, you have to be completely honest when writing your Success and Failure Scenarios. You have to be very detailed. You have to be real. This isn't something to gloss over, or do quickly. It's not a one-liner or quick synopsis — this is a very important part of your reaching the goals you desire. You should feel real emotion as you're creating them.

When I'm teaching these techniques in person, it's common to have most of the room crying as they are writing their scenarios, both tears of joy when writing the Success Scenarios and tears of sorrow when writing the Failure Scenarios. If you're feeling that emotion, it means you're doing it right.

Emotion, not fact, is the driver of all action.

Each one of us is driven by emotion. We may read facts or data, but it's not until we have an emotional reaction to them that we'll take action. Keeping this in mind, it's very important, when reading your scenarios, that you truly concentrate on what they're saying. You need to actually feel the emotion caused by these scenarios for them to inspire you to succeed.

Here's the true power in it: Either one of these pages could be your reality! As you read each page, you realize, "This could be my life!" That aspect of your life could be really good, because you met that goal — or really bad, because you didn't. If, for example, your goal is to have a happy relationship, imagine exactly what that looks like and exactly how it feels.

In fact, take a moment right now to think about your significant other, or someone you're very close to. Picture their face smiling at you right now. Really—if you haven't done so, please stop reading, and picture them right now.

How do you feel inside right now? You probably have a very warm feeling inside, and perhaps even have a smile on your face as well! You feel drawn to that. That's a carrot for you, and some of the power of the Success Scenario.

Now, take a moment again, and picture that person crying, with you to blame for it, and them looking at you with disgust. Again, please stop reading and take the time to do this.

How do you feel now? If you really took the time to do this exercise, you probably feel pretty rotten right now. This is a feeling you'd take action to avoid. And, if you are like most people, you'd do just about anything to avoid it. That's the power of the Failure Scenario.

We've all heard stories of people performing seemingly superhuman feats to keep something terrible from happening: the mother lifting a car to free her trapped child; the dad whose son is being attacked by a bear fighting him off with a piece of wood; the elderly lady fighting off an attacker with a cane. My own mother, elderly and alone in our house, scared off an intruder who was climbing through the window in the middle of the night—with her hands!

The main driving motivation was the fear of loss: If they didn't take action, someone they loved, or they themselves, would die. That fear can be a powerful force in helping you accomplish great and important things, if it's used in a positive manner.

It's important to point out that, in the long run, I believe that there's no such thing as complete failure, because you can always learn something and move on. With that in mind, you might wonder why I call these "Failure Scenarios."

In this case, it is a failure to reach a specific stated goal because we are talking about a finite unit of time and a specific experience.

For instance, if a marriage ends in divorce, I'm going to call it a failed marriage, no matter what the reason. Can you learn from it, and apply that knowledge to future success? You bet.

And that's what will make you a success in the long run. In fact, as you saw in the previous chapter, I believe the understanding of failure is so important that I devoted an entire chapter in this book to it.

I again quote Michael Jordan, the great basketball player, who says:

"I can accept failure; everyone fails at
something. But I can't accept not trying."

There is a fine line that needs to be walked on this subject, though. I believe it may be true that what we focus on, we achieve, both good and bad. If we focus too much on the potential of failure, we can actually be inviting failure by putting that picture too deeply into our minds.

On the other hand, it's important to remember that the fear of loss is a greater motivator than the prospect of gain. Why? We often become more emotional about the potential of losing something than we do of gaining something, and it's emotion that drives us more than anything else.

For example, the thought of my children growing up to be happy, healthy adults is a very motivating one for me. I work hard daily to help ensure that. But the thought of one of them getting hurt or worse is extremely emotional to me. I would do almost anything to keep that from happening, including die for them. Talk about a great motivator!

Therefore, if we look only at the Success Scenario, we're missing out on a potentially larger motivating force. All too often, people don't reach their goals because they're focusing only on the prospect of gain, and missing out on that larger motivating force of "What happens if I don't reach my goal?"

They attempt to ignore that possibility until it becomes a reality and can no longer be ignored. In the meantime, they've failed to harness the very force that could have helped them avoid failure and propelled them to success: the fear of loss.

So, what's our solution to the conundrum of not wanting negative thoughts to impair our ability to succeed, yet harnessing their power to motivate us?

That's why it's so important that when reading your three pages twice a day, you begin by reading the Failure Scenario. That will engrain in your subconscious the need to take the action that you'll read next in your Action Plan. At the end of your Failure Scenario, you will write the following:

> MY FUTURE WILL BE DIFFERENT. I HAVE THE POWER TO ENSURE MY SUCCESS SCENARIO BECOMES MY NEW REALITY. I WILL DO THE FOLLOWING TO MAKE SURE I SUCCEED IN REACHING MY GOAL.

Then, read each step on your Action Plan, and visualize how you'll accomplish each of the points today to move toward your desired outcome: your Success Scenario.

Finally, conclude by reading the Success Scenario to cement in your mind that, if you will take the actions you need to take throughout the day, success will be the ultimate achievement. Then, at the end of your Success Scenario, write,

> THIS IS MY FUTURE. I WILL DO WHATEVER IT TAKES TO MAKE THIS HAPPEN. TODAY, I WILL TAKE THE ACTIONS IN MY PLAN SO I MAY ENJOY THE HAPPINESS I DESERVE.

As a result, your Success Scenario will be your lasting picture that you'll move toward every single day.

For example, if you have a short-term goal of saving enough money to buy a car, your Failure Scenario might be:

> I'm still driving the same old car, wondering if it will start, and praying that it will stay running if it does. I'm embarrassed to drive this rust-bucket because even though no one says anything bad about it, I know what they're

thinking. Driving in the winter time is so treacherous that I only leave the house if I absolutely have to. Forget road trips; I'm not convinced it will make it across town.

MY FUTURE WILL BE DIFFERENT. I HAVE THE POWER TO ENSURE MY SUCCESS SCENARIO BECOMES MY NEW REALITY. I WILL DO THE FOLLOWING TO MAKE SURE I SUCCEED IN REACHING MY GOAL.

Your Success Scenario could read something like:

I have saved up the money I need to buy my new-to- me car. I'm incredibly excited to walk into the dealership to pick it out. When the salesman starts talking about financing, I smile at him and say, 'I'll be paying cash today.' As I get in and drive off, I feel the sense of accomplishment of reaching a goal, and driving a car that I can be proud of.

I know it will be reliable, and I can finally feel confident taking any road trip I want. It will be a joy to drive in the winter, knowing that I and those riding with me will be as safe as possible. I feel very proud of myself for accomplishing this goal, and knowing I truly deserve this beautiful car, because I sacrificed and earned it.

THIS IS MY FUTURE. I WILL DO WHATEVER IT TAKES TO MAKE THIS HAPPEN. TODAY, I WILL TAKE THE ACTIONS IN MY PLAN SO I MAY ENJOY THE HAPPINESS I DESERVE.

This leads directly to the Action Plan that we will discuss in the next chapter.

Before we get to that, here is the big question:

What do you do if you don't take the actions in your Action Plan and find your Failure Scenario as your new temporary reality?

If you can't answer this question yourself right now, please go back and re-read the chapter on Embracing Failure!

The quick answer: You try again. And again. And again. And again.

Failure is nothing but the temporary effect of not reaching your goals the first time.

You need to be completely honest with yourself about why you didn't succeed this time. Don't blame something or someone else; take responsibility. If it was, in part, truly due to some factors that were out of your control, write down a new Action Plan that is within your control.

Next, take a close look at your Success Scenario: Why is this important to you? Your last Success Scenario might not have been truly emotional enough to you to get you to take the correct actions on a daily basis to achieve it. Apparently, the things that kept you from succeeding were more important at that moment.

Perhaps your Failure Scenario didn't provide enough of a "stick." You need to have a complete heart-to-heart with yourself.

But know this: Failure is only temporary. It may not feel like it, but it is.

Hope is never lost. It may feel like it, but it's not.

Most people who have achieved greatness have been on the edge of despair at some point in their lives. The same thoughts went through their heads that may go through yours.

Abraham Lincoln, the Wright brothers, Bill Gates, Nelson Mandela, George Washington, Alexander Graham Bell, Thomas Edison — the list could go on and on. And all of them had come to despair in their lives at one point where they thought about giving up. Their fire had faded to naught but a glimmer.

But because they gathered their strength, and fanned that last spark of hope, it grew into a radiance that would change the lives of generations around the world long after they were gone. Their light still burns today (especially Edison's). Even you have been touched by their radiance. Those achievements would be missing from your life if they had thought of failure as permanent. Thankfully, they did not — and you shouldn't either!

As Confucius said,

"Our greatest glory is not in never falling, but
in rising every time we fall."

The world will cheer a victor who has overcome great odds and continued to forge a new path through the jungle of adversity. It will ignore a silver-spooned imposter who has never seen the trial of fire, who does not know the sting of hardship and the pain of failure, which only experience can bring.

Failure is merely a stepping stone to success.

You are merely experiencing what you must experience to reach your goals.

No one said it would be easy, but it will certainly be worth it!

If you question that right now, go back to your Success and Failure Scenarios, and visualize them using all of your senses and the passion you originally wrote them with.

Then you'll remember how you feel about that and why you must, and you will, move forward — because you emotionally value it and want it so intensely!

SELF-EXAMINATION QUESTION: Think of one aspect of your life: Your finances, your health, or your closest relationship. Look forward several years into the future. What's the worst possible scenario? What's the best possible scenario. Is the worst case scenario bad enough to make you WANT to take action so your best case scenario comes true?

CHAPTER 9

Sacrifice Now, or Sacrifice Forever

"You can't achieve anything in life without a small amount of sacrifice."

— Dr. Martin Luther King, Jr.

I once began working with a coaching client, and quickly realized he wasn't willing to actually do what it took to reach his goals. He didn't want to change; didn't want to put in the actual work, and wasn't willing to sacrifice anything. He wasn't just a dreamer, he was a 'wisher'. He wished everything would go his way, but wasn't willing to do what it took. Needless to say, he wasn't my client for long. I let him know that there wasn't I or anyone else could do to help him, until he was ready to help himself.

Until you realize you're going to have to sacrifice, you're not ready to begin your journey.

When I'm going backpacking, there's only so much gear I can take if I want to reach my destination. We have a saying in the backpacking world: ounces equals pounds, pounds equals miles. In other words, all the little ounces add up to pounds, and the more pounds you have, the less distance you're going to be able to travel.

And that's too bad, because there's things I'd really like to have! Extra changes of clothing, extra food, okay, whiskey; but my favorite: a Dutch oven!

No, for you younger crowd, stop giggling; A Dutch oven is something used to cook over a fire, and usually made out of cast iron.

Man, there is NOTHING like a peach cobbler made in a Dutch oven when you're out in the woods! But that's not all! It's like a real oven – you can make anything in it! Imagine hot biscuits and gravy on a cold morning, or even a Cornish game hen!

But here's the problem with that: It's heavy! Trying to take it with me would weigh me down! If my goal is to summit a mountain – there's no way I'm doing it keeping ahold of this – no matter how much I want it, or think I deserve it! When I'm deciding what gear I'm going to take with me, I have to sacrifice. I have to leave my Dutch oven behind.

And it's the same way with you and your goals.

You're reading this book because you have your own journey to take – you have your own mountain to climb!

And if YOU want to be successful, you're going to have to sacrifice! Listen: there's no such thing as success without sacrifice!

It may be something you really want to take with you! It may be something you really like, or is actually important to you (like another goal or a cause), but whether your goal has to do with money, success in business, your health, or even your marriage, let's face it: you're going to have to sacrifice!

And that shouldn't surprise you: You've probably heard the saying: If you always do what you've always done, you'll always get what you've always got! For things to change, you have to change. And your habits have to change.

But in truth, it's even worse than that! If you always do what you've always done, you WON'T always get what you've always got! You're going to get less!

The world isn't staying the same.

There's no such thing as status quo. If you're not moving forward, you're moving backward.

For instance, let's talk about your health. The good news is: You're getting older! (the alternative isn't so good...)

But along with that, your body isn't staying the same – it's changing! Your metabolism is slowing down, your bone density is degrading, and on and on!

If you always eat what you always ate, you're not going to get what you always got: You're not going to stay the same weight: you're going to gain weight. If you stay at the same activity level that you have, (in other words, don't exercise) you're body isn't going to stay the same. You're going to lose muscle mass. You're going to gain weight.

Financially, if you always do what you've always done, your finances won't stay the same. Each year, your money is worth less and less. You used to be able to buy a loaf of bread for a nickel – you can't any more. And every day, you're getting closer to retirement age, if you're not there already.

In business, everything is changing every single day, from technology to best practices. And let's face it: Someone else is entering your profession who is hungry, and driven, and willing to make the sacrifices others aren't willing to – and those are the people who are going to reach the top.

You need to do different to have different.

If we're talking about your marriage, you're certainly going to have to sacrifice! Don't think so? 50% of the marriages end in divorce. And most of those 50% are made up of people who thought they'd get their way every time, and didn't want to sacrifice!

There's no such thing as a magic pill. There's no such thing as get rich quick. You have to work, and that means you have to sacrifice. Maybe your time, maybe your pride, maybe your sanity! But you're going to have to sacrifice. You're going to have to leave your Dutch oven behind.

And in marriage, it may be having the tough, but gentle and loving, conversations that build communications, understanding, and trust. And it's certainly going to involve making concessions in your life!

In business, you're going to have to do things you don't want to do, when you don't feel like doing them! The refusal to do so is YOUR Dutch oven!

So, if you're not willing to put together an action plan with the steps that will actually get you to your goal in the timeline you want it to, it doesn't matter how frightening you write your Failure Scenario, you don't really mean it.

What you're really saying is "I'm only willing to avoid that Failure Scenario if I don't have to sacrifice too much; if I'm able to keep doing the things I want to do."

And no matter how beautiful your Success Scenario is, what you're really saying is "I only want that if I don't have to sacrifice too much to get it."

So, if you're not willing to do what it takes, you need to change your goal!

Look, I could take my Dutch oven with me, and camp somewhere just a little ways down the trail, maybe a nice stream somewhere. But a nice stream isn't my goal. My goal is the summit, the top of the mountain.

And that's what your goal is, too! If you just wanted to go a short distance, you wouldn't be reading this book. But you made the decision to go to the top, whatever that is for you.

So make those sacrifices. Whether it's for your health, for your marriage, for your business or finances, you're going to HAVE to sacrifice! The truth is: You WANT to sacrifice, so you can leave behind the things, or practices, that would weigh you down and keep you from reaching your goal.

So what are your Dutch ovens?

Your homework for this chapter is to write down a list of the sacrifices you're going to make so you can reach YOUR goal! That's right – write them down. Because doing so you're actually making a commitment to yourself to do what it takes to make sure your Failure Scenario does not become your future, and your Success Scenario does!

And then, leave your Dutch ovens behind, and enjoy your journey to the top!

SELF-EXAMINATION QUESTION: Be very honest with yourself: What are you going to have to sacrifice to reach your goals? Is it worth it?

CHAPTER 10

Steps to Change Your Life: Developing Your Action Plan

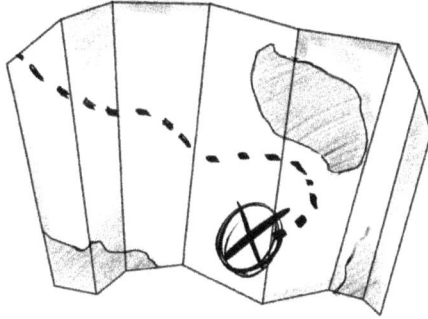

*All you need is the plan, the road map, and the
courage to press on to your destination.*

— Earl Nightingale

You can have all the motivation in the world, but if you don't have an Action Plan, nothing will change.

NASA doesn't attempt to launch a rocket without a detailed guidance plan. You can have literally tons of force powering that rocket, but without a proper guidance system, who knows where it will end up? If you put the wrong address in your GPS, you're not going to get where you want to go, no matter how motivated you are to get there.

The Action Plan is where you identify your detailed, step-by-step strategy. These are the specific actions you will need to take on a daily basis to reach your goal.

This is where the transformation occurs that decides which reality will become yours: the one on the left, or the one on the right—your Failure Scenario or your Success Scenario. These are the steps you have complete control over, that will determine your ultimate success or failure.

Sound intense? It is. It has the power to change lives, as well as destinies. It has the power to change futures, and history. Most importantly, it has the power to change *you*.

The players in our football scenario in Chapter 5 developed their Action Plan:

"Conditioning before school. We all have to be there. No excuses."

"At lunch, we need to quiz each other on plays."

"And we need to watch what we eat better. Cut down on the junk. We need every edge we can get."

"And at practice, all of us need to give absolutely everything we've got. No more goofing around for half the time we're out there. At the end, we need to crawl back to the locker room because we used all our energy on the field. All in or nothing at all."

Remember the farmer in the Oxcart parable? He knew he had to build a bridge, but he wasn't sure how, so he found professional help. I can't emphasize this step enough. He could have attempted to build a bridge on his own, but that might not have worked well, and I'm not sure oxen are the best swimmers.

I recommend getting experts' input on any of your points on these sheets. If I want to know how to best keep my marriage in good shape, I'll talk to the experts: marriage counselors and people I know who have a great marriage. I may even talk to those who have failed, to learn from mistakes they have made.

If I want to do the best I can with my investment dollars, I'll talk to a financial advisor and other successful people. If my goal is success on a certain project, I'll talk to experts in that field, get their advice, and use it as part of my personalized plan.

Depending on the nature of your goal, this can merely be someone who has built additional income streams, or lost weight and kept it off, or is more successful than you in your industry. The more good advice you have, the better. If your goal includes another person, such as saving a relationship, it's best to work with them, as well.

I've found that if you ask people for advice, they're almost always very happy to help. The Internet can be a great resource as well, but make sure it's written by actual experts and not just someone with an opinion. Without expert advice, you might take steps you think will help, but which may truly turn out to be counterproductive!

So just how do you go about writing your Action Plan?

To begin with, you'll want to be very specific about every action that takes you either toward, or away from, your goal, and there may be many of them. Remember, you have to write this. It has to come from your head, and your heart. You can't just take someone else's Action Plan and cut and paste it to be your own.

I'm going to give you several examples in this book, but you can't just adopt these as your own. You might include many of the points, but it all has to be from your point of view, or it will remain foreign to you—not something your conscious and your subconscious mind— can own.

Additionally, each point must be put in positive terms. If you have negative points, or "bad" actions, written down, your mind will focus on those bad actions. For example, instead of having "infidelity" as one of the obstacles to a happy marriage, you'd want to write down, "I will always be faithful to my spouse in every way."

Continuing with the example of buying a car, from the last chapter, an Action Plan might be:

- I will put at least $300 per month into my car savings account.
- I'll work 5 extra hours per week at my job.
- I'll cut my latte stops to once every two weeks—I can enjoy regular coffee at home and at work.
- I'll set my home thermostat to 63 degrees in the winter, and not use the air conditioner in the summer, if I can help it.
- I'll take my lunch to work each day, and not buy fast food.
- We'll eat out as a family only twice per month.
- At the end of each week, I'll monitor how it's going, and adjust my plan to either save more money if I need to, or work fewer hours if I don't need to.

That's it—it's as simple as that!

Keep in mind that you may not develop a perfect, or even very good, plan your first time. Each of these is a fluid document that can be changed as you think of new ideas. Feel free to add to them, subtract from them, or start all over from scratch. You own this. There is no right or wrong —there's only what works for you.

As a reminder, at the bottom of the Action Plan you want to draw two joined arrows: one that faces left toward where your Failure Scenario will be posted, and one that faces right toward your Success Scenario. This will give you the visual indication that your action or inaction will take you one direction or the other, and help ensure you do what you're supposed to do every single day.

As you are reading your scenarios and Action Plan twice a day, you'll analyze how well you've done in accomplishing each step: Did yesterday bring you closer to your Failure Scenario on the left, or to your Success Scenario on the right? Which direction will today take you?

When doing personal coaching, I'll often have partners tell me, "Well, yesterday was more of a Left Day (referring to the Failure Plan to the left), but today will be a Right Day." Does this really work? You bet it does!

Do it for 90 days, and you'll be amazed by the results!

As the great orator and author Charles Swindoll says,

"Life is 10% what happens to me and 90% how I react to it."

Now, let's identify which areas of your life you'd like to improve!

SELF-EXAMINATION QUESTION: In the goal that you're going to work on first, what are the top 3 best places to go to find out the daily actions you'll need to take to reach them?

CHAPTER 11

Tune Up

"No matter how good you get you can always get better, and that's the exciting part."

— Tiger Woods

Once you have your oxcart completed, I want to give you full permission to change it completely. In fact, I guarantee you that you're going to change it, and it's critical that you do.

See, sometimes people start off with their Oxcart working wonderfully, but eventually find the excuses creeping in again. Over time, they find they're not completing all of the points on their daily action plan; they're doing some of it, and they feel that's okay. Or they get busy one morning. They're rushing out the door. They got up late, so they don't have time to read their Oxcart, and they don't get that inspirational hit in the morning, or they're just too tired at night to do it. Their life got busy, and they got distracted. Maybe they went on vacation. They got out of the habit, and before long, they're not doing it at all.

The excuses begin to make sense. They seem valid. But remember: There's only 2 things: excuses and results. If it's not a result, it's merely an excuse, and your goals don't care what your excuses are!

Let me say that again. It's important this hits home.

> *There's only 2 things, excuses and results.*
> *If it's not a result, it's merely an excuse, and your*
> *goals don't care what your excuses are.*

Again, this may be hardcore, but it's the truth.

And if you let it slide, the self-doubt may creep into your head, "well, maybe the Oxcart Technique just doesn't work for me. Maybe it's just something else I tried, and it didn't work, so I think I'll give up."

Let me tell you right now, that is not the case. You need to hear this: The Oxcart Technique has been proven time and time again with all sorts of people, from all sorts of different backgrounds, and personality types, and everything else. There's zero question in my mind that it can and will work for you. But just like a fine running car needs a tune up on a recurring basis, so does your Oxcart Technique. And just like you should do preventative maintenance on your car before it starts running badly, you need to do the same here.

So how do you do it? Well, consider this chapter your tune up manual. As you know, there are really only 3 main parts to the technique:

Number 1, your Failure Scenario. Most of the time when I work with people whose initial plan isn't working for them, it's because they haven't attached enough emotion to their Failure Scenario. Remembering that emotion, not fact, is the driver of all action, there must be significant emotion tied to your Failure Scenario to make you uncomfortable enough to push you out of your comfort zone!

I find they haven't driven down deep enough to what failure really means, not so much to themselves, because often they don't care so much about themselves, but to the other people who will really be affected: to their spouse, to their children, their employees, and so on.

So I'm going to ask you right now to go read your Failure Scenario that you've set up. Does it include the harsh truth about what will happen to those you care about if you fail? Here's a litmus test for you if it's effective enough: Did you get emotional reading it? I mean really emotional. If not, you need to dig further. Please understand, I'm not trying to be cruel here. I'm trying to be honest. It does you no good if I sugarcoat anything.

I want to make sure that you have the full impact that this Failure Scenario could truly not only be your future, but the future of others who are impacted by it as well. What you do every day in your action plan, or you don't do, affects more people than just you, doesn't it? And if you truly internalize that, it'll propel you like nothing else can because odds are, if you're here, you are a caring person. You probably care about others more than even yourself if you're here, and that may help really propel you.

So take another look at your Failure Scenario. Does reading it bring up strong emotions? Does it make you almost want to cry, or bring out the 'fight' in you? Does it make you emphatically say "There's no way in the world I'm going to let that happen! I'll do whatever it takes to make sure it doesn't! And, of course, "whatever it takes" is the steps you've written in your Daily Action Plan!

If your Failure Scenario doesn't elicit these reactions, you need to give it a tune up. Make sure it's strong enough to drive you; to make you want to stick to your daily action plan no matter what excuses try to get in the way, or fears or self-doubts try to hold you back.

The next step: your Action Plan.

Is your daily Action Plan achievable or did you bite off more than you can chew? Understand that it's normal for people to do exactly that. They get all excited and put a too much in their daily Action Plan; more than they can actually do during their day with their schedules. The phrase "shoot for the moon. Even if you miss, you'll land among the stars" does not apply here. You only write in your plan the action you WILL take, every single day; not just on your good days. Remember: this is a marathon, not a sprint. And remember: these aren't daily goals. They're absolutes. Things you will absolutely do no matter what tries to get in the way.

There's no harm at all in adjusting your daily Action Plan down to something you can and absolutely will do every single day. In fact, it's critical.

The next important point on your Action Plan: Is each point completely and totally in your control? For instance, contacting three new prospects a day and doing three 'follow-ups' is within my control. That can be on my Action Plan. Whether they actually buy from me is not in my control at all, so 'sell to three customers' can't be on my plan. For example, if you're a realtor, you can't control how many listings you'll get. Your Action Plan can't say 'get 5 new listings a week.' That's not within your control. You can only control how many people you'll contact, so 'contact 20 new FSBOs (For Sale By Owner listings) each day' is perfectly fine. The numbers will take care of themselves. You probably already know the odds and what the numbers are in whatever industry you're in, and can adjust your daily actions according to that.

If you have an action on your plan that's outside of your control or more than you can handle on a consistent basis, you'll want to tune it up.

Finally, take a look at your Success Scenario.

Are those the things that truly motivate you? Or are you trying to buy off from somebody else's dream? Again, early in my business career, I was told to put pictures of a big house, a fancy car, pictures of beaches, and all those kind of things on a 'dream board', so that's what I did.

Here's the problem. I don't care about any of those things. I'm my happiest in a tent, in some harsh environment in the world somewhere, with no one around for miles and miles.

Those positive visualizations, or Success Scenarios, didn't work for me. First of all, I don't care about those things, so they're simply not a motivating factor for me. They weren't worth me getting out of my comfort zone for and taking the daily actions I needed to take! Secondly, coming from my background and 'never expected to grow up to be anything', I never believed they'd happen to a 'guy like me', so my self-doubts kept me from taking action. Once I realized this and refined my Success Scenario, it began actually helping me reach my goals.

And keep in mind, often we'll do more for others than we'll do for ourselves. Recently, when I was representing all of Boy Scouts of America in my scoutmaster uniform on a survival reality show, my Success Scenario and Failure Scenario had nothing to do with me. It had everything to do with the scouts in my troop, and the look of pride if I did well, or disappointment if I didn't. Both of those visualizations, the carrot and the stick coupled together, pushed me through all of the hardships and discomforts, self-doubts and fears, and all the excuses I could come up with being the oldest person on the entire show, competing against special forces guys and military survival instructors!

Read your Success Scenario again. How does it make you feel?

Do you find yourself smiling without realizing it? Does it make your heart feel good? Maybe even make you want to stop reading this and get into immediate action? If not, it's not strong enough. It doesn't create enough emotion. Instead, think about those things that are truly worth working for and getting through the challenges for and fighting for. Those are the elements of a good success scenario.

Now that you've tuned up your Oxcart Technique, you need to evaluate your own actions. In fact, this is where most people fall short on the technique, so fall short on reaching their goals.

The complete power of the Oxcart Technique lies in reading your Failure Scenario, your Action Plan, and your Success Scenario out loud in that order once in the morning to focus you on your goals for the day, then in the evening to gauge how you did that day. This is where the power is.

As the immortal Zig Ziglar said:

> *"It was character that got us out of bed, commitment that moved us into action, and discipline that enabled us to follow through."*

Your discipline with this technique will govern your discipline toward reaching your goals.

When you read your pages, are you truly focusing, concentrating, visualizing what they're saying or merely skimming through them to get through the exercise and move on to other things? Are you actually thinking of something else while you're doing it?

You have to be completely focused here for it to be effective: visualizing it, internalizing it, actually being there mentally. Keep in mind that either one of those Failure or Success Scenarios can and will be your future depending on the actions that you take or don't take every single day. This is important, and it's critical that you treat it this way.

Remember, emotion, not fact, is the driver of all action. We can read all the facts in the world, but until we have an emotional response to them, it means absolutely nothing.

It's this full commitment to the action that will get you the results you're looking for, but to get the results you're looking for, you have to make the commitment!

If all you did was read this book and get the knowledge from it but didn't take the actions, you wouldn't be much better off than if you didn't read the book at all. Think of it this way:

If you knew how to weld, but didn't actually weld, or only did it part way, would the two pieces of metal hold together? Absolutely not.

If you built a detailed route for an epic journey, then, when setting off, threw away the maps and GPS, and decided to just hope for the best, would you reach your destination? Probably not.

And yet that's what too many people do when working toward their goals. They want the rewards without the daily effort required to reach them!

Think of it as exercising – If you don't do it every day, you won't build that muscle. In fact, your muscle would atrophy, and you'll go backward.

This is your psychological workout. Your motivational workout. This is your success workout! This is the deciding factor as to which will be your future: Your Failure Scenario or your Success Scenario.

Fine tune your Oxcart Technique continuously, take the actions, and build the future that most people only dream of.

CHAPTER 12

Identifying Your Goals

Definiteness of purpose is the starting point of all achievement.

— W. Clement Stone

It's time to identify your goals so you can begin the process of achieving them through your Success Scenarios.

Every single person has a different purpose in reading this book, or most likely several. It's time to narrow down your focus to some achievable goals, and get to work making them become your reality!

Please read each of these carefully and consider how they apply to you:

Would you like to inspire your team members to perform at levels they may never have before?

Is your marriage the best it could possibly be? Do you feel as close to your spouse as you did the first day you were married—or even closer? Would you like to make it the happiest it could possibly be?

Would you like to double the size of an organization, whether it's a club you're a part of or your company?

Would you like to lose 20, 50, or 100 pounds?

Would you like to earn more money, starting right now?

Do you have a retirement nest egg big enough to support you in comfort during your Golden Years? Would you like to grow it considerably, regardless of your income?

Are you having relationship challenges with someone you live with, work with, or somehow interact with in your life? Who comes to mind? Would it improve your life to mend those relationships, at least somewhat?

Do you have members of your team who are having challenges getting along?

Is there an addiction you are having trouble overcoming—perhaps time-wasting, smoking, pornography, alcohol, or others? Do you know someone else who is?

Would you like to be more successful in your job, profession, or business?

Is there another goal, either short-term or long-term, that you'd like to achieve? It can be anything from buying a car or becoming more physically fit, to discovering a cure for a disease or peace between nations! (Yes, seriously!)

Look back at the list above. Which of these areas would you like to improve on, starting now?

Before you read on, take a moment and imagine having success in those areas. Actually visualize your achievement. How incredible will that feel?

I have great news for you: The following chapters in this book are going to give you step-by-step instructions to achieve every single one of those goals, and many, many more.

Is it worth the time and effort it will take?

The great Dalai Lama once said,

"Happiness is not something readymade.
It comes from your own actions."

Whatever your goal might be, The Oxcart Technique will help you achieve it. Whatever you can imagine that needs improvement, can be improved.

It's said that a dream plus action equals reality. The challenge is often keeping up the passion to maintain the burning desire to take action on a daily basis without losing steam.

The solution is in your hands, literally.

If you'll take the actions outlined in this book, your goals and dreams really can come true!

The next few chapters will take you through specific categories in which most people would like to improve. Whether or not each of them applies to you, I'd recommend reading them, as each of them will contain some information that will help you hone your skills in The Oxcart Technique.

Additionally, as you're reading these chapters, you may think of someone you know who could also benefit from the information in it!

Now, try to avoid the temptation of starting on several goals at the same time. Too many priorities at once can distract you and water down your results. Start with one or two until you feel comfortable with your success in those areas, and then move on to those further down on your list.

As the inspirational author Denis Waitley says,

"The reason most people never reach their goals is that they don't define them, or ever seriously consider them as believable or achievable. Winners can tell you where they are going, what they plan to do along the way, and who will be sharing the adventure with them."

You have defined your goals. Now it's time to achieve them.

SELF-EXAMINATION QUESTION: What aspect of your life are you going to change forever by taking the actions you're about to learn?

APPLICATION

WEALTH

CHAPTER 13

Taking Your Job, Profession, or Business to New Heights

*The more you lose yourself in something bigger than
yourself, the more energy you will have.*

— Norman Vincent Peale

The business battlefield is littered with bodies of people who have attempted to reach goals over and over again, and eventually given up. You may be one of them, or know someone who is. We all do.

The great news is — The Oxcart Technique can greatly multiply your chances of success, and your degree of success, turning you from a casualty to a conqueror!

In fact, success in business is one of the most popular topics of all the ones that I teach.

In this chapter, we are going to discuss how to apply The Oxcart Technique to help you succeed in several different types of businesses. From attorneys to zookeepers, these methods will translate into pretty much every job, profession, or business on the face of the earth!

Regardless of the type of endeavor, there are several universal truths, and you have a considerably better chance of success if you apply these principles.

In so doing, we're going to harness every ounce of power and passion you have in your innermost being, and use it to help propel you through the barriers toward the success of your dreams.

Sound good?

I realize that's a bold statement — but it's also completely true!

Many people set professional goals but aren't truly focused on the force that will propel them forward — on the why, as in "Why should I? What do I care enough about in life that will make me yearn to do whatever it takes to reach that goal? What would be a Success Scenario that would drive me to accomplish the daily tasks to achieve those goals and dreams?"

Perhaps an even more important element that's usually left out: "Why must I?" What is the stick that is so unpleasant in your mind, that you absolutely must follow your Action Plan to avoid the potential of that pain? What if you don't reach your goal? What difference will that make in your life, or in the lives of others who depend on your success?

For example, if you're a Realtor, the Success Scenario can't simply be, "I will sell 100 more houses this year." Granted, selling 100 more houses this year is your bottom-line goal, but it's not emotional. It won't drive you. It doesn't make you want to rush out there and make it happen.

If you're a business owner or CEO and you set a goal to increase your company's bottom line by 20% or your stock price by 500%, that's nifty — but what's your driving force? What will inspire you to make it happen?

If you're in sales and want to advance to the top, that sounds great. But what "happy thought" will keep you going when you hit your 100th "No"?

If you are an employee, merely working for the paycheck will make you someone who is easily replaced, especially by another who is passionate about doing their job, because they're driven to excel by their Success and Failure Scenarios.

Simply saying, "I'll make more money" won't do it, either. You can't get passionate about money. You can get passionate about what it can do for you or for others.

Money is not an end.

But it is a means to achieve many desirable ends.

So what if you make more money? What will that money do for you? What difference will it make in your life? What difference will it make in your family's life? Would it be of interest to travel together, or buy that extra home you've always dreamed of, or that jet, or that island?

How about something a little more down-to-earth, like, say, paying your bills and getting out of debt, with the extravagance of having a little extra money left over at the end of the month?

Or would it be beneficial for a charitable cause that's important to you? Specifically, what will happen as a result of your charitable giving? Will more children around the world be able to read, or simply not starve to death, because you were able to donate more money due to your extra business efforts? Will you help fund a cure for a disease that has struck someone you know? Will the world be, in some way, a better place because you reached your business goal?

Perhaps it is simply the thrill of the challenge, the exhilaration of reaching new heights, or a sense of pride. Your reason may be the same as that of George Mallory, a Mount Everest pioneer, when he explained his need to climb to the summit, "Because it's there... Everest is the highest mountain in the world, and no man has reached its summit. Its existence is a challenge. The answer is instinctive, in part, I suppose, of man's desire to conquer the universe."

If the income isn't important, then what is? Why should you take time away from your family, friends, or hobbies to do this? Is it a sense of accomplishment that will drive you to reach new heights?

If you are a Realtor, is it that you know you'll help 100 more families find their dream home, without any of the pitfalls that occur with less experienced agents, or worse, no Realtor at all? What carrot will drive you when challenges, apathy, or procrastination start to slow you down?

What benefit comes from it? How does it affect your life, or your family's lives, or the lives of others, short term or long term?

Does the additional income enable you to leave a larger legacy to be remembered by after you're gone?

How about the lives of your employees? How will they be affected if you grow your bottom line by 20%?

If you're already a top agent with plenty of income, there might not be that much of a downside. It may be the Success Scenario, rather than the Failure Scenario, that drives you the most.

On the other hand, if sales have not been going so well and you're having trouble making the payments on your own house, the Failure Scenario may be pretty easy to write, and to be a particularly motivating force.

For the business owner or CEO example from above, what happens if you don't reach those lofty goals? Again, if you're already financially set, your answer might be "Not much." The prospect of gain may be a much bigger motivator than the fear of loss. But perhaps if you try hard, you may be able to come up with some very compelling issues. For instance, if there's a charitable cause that the additional income would have gone to, what will happen to the people, places or animals that won't be getting that money, after all? What does that look like?

If the company doesn't continue to grow, what could happen to it in today's competitive environment? What could happen to your employees? Perhaps it's merely a matter of pride, knowing that you didn't grow the company as you envisioned, and falling short of your goals just won't do for you!

When talking with large groups of employees and business owners, I ask the question, "What aspects of your job or business are the most important to you?"

As you can imagine, the answers are many and varied. Certain answers, however, come up the most. The top nine important aspects of your job/business are:

- Being able to control aspects of my job or work environment
- Job security
- Relationships with my coworkers
- Money
- Opportunity to use my skills
- Opportunities for advancement
- The feeling I'm making a difference at my job or in the world
- Recognition/Appreciation
- Feeling that I and my opinion are valued

Considering your personal situation, which three from the list above would be the most important to you?

When writing your Success and Failure Scenarios, you'll want to focus mainly on those three areas.

For example, let's say that Money, Opportunities for advancement, Recognition/Appreciation were your top three choices.

Your Success Scenario, in part, might be:

> I have reached the 10 Million Dollar Club and am so proud to walk across the stage at our annual banquet in front of the entire company.
>
> My brand-new Porsche Boxster is waiting for me outside to take my wife and me to the airport for that dream vacation we've always wanted: to visit Paris in the spring, First Class all the way.
>
> When we get back, I'll start my new job as Director of Sales for the entire Northeastern Region, with the new office and income that go with it.
>
> THIS IS MY FUTURE. I WILL DO WHATEVER IT TAKES TO MAKE THIS HAPPEN. TODAY, I WILL TAKE THE ACTIONS IN MY PLAN SO I MAY ENJOY THE HAPPINESS I DESERVE.

Sounds fun, doesn't it? It does, if those things are important to you. If they're not important to you, then they wouldn't be a driving force at all.

On the other hand, if Job security, Opportunity to use my skills, the feeling I'm making a difference at my job or in the world are your top three choices from the list, your Success Scenario would be more focused on those areas:

> Even with the economy's ups and downs, I'm still safe in my job, getting to do what I love: creating things that are used around the world. My retirement plan is in place to allow Brenda and me to travel throughout the country, building houses for Habitat for Humanity, seeing the looks on those families' faces when they see their new home and the new start that comes with it.

> THIS IS MY FUTURE. I WILL DO WHATEVER IT TAKES TO MAKE THIS HAPPEN. TODAY, I WILL TAKE THE ACTIONS IN MY PLAN SO I MAY ENJOY THE HAPPINESS I DESERVE.

These are two very different Success Scenarios that are inspiring to those who wrote them. Interestingly, each of these people might find the other's Success Scenario completely boring. That's why it's so important to focus on what truly motivates you, personally.

The Failure Scenarios should be equally individualized to you, depending on what you have to lose from being unsuccessful at reaching your goals the first time.

When talking with the same group of employees and business owners mentioned earlier, I asked the question, "What are the things you most fear about being stuck in the same job that you don't like, for whatever reason, for a long period of time?"

Again, their answers were as varied as their personalities and situations:

- I won't be making enough money.
- I just won't care about my job any more. I will have lost the passion I once had.
- I will still be working too many hours and won't ever have time for things that are important to me.
- Feeling like I've hit a dead end, with nowhere to advance to from here.

- My environment would never change: I'd come to work every day to the same office and stare at the same four walls.
- I don't want to work for the same jerk anymore.
- I'm still treading water at the office, barely getting by. It doesn't feel like I'm really getting anywhere.
- Too much red tape, paperwork, and hoops to jump through.
- Working with the same people I'm bickering with already.
- I won't feel challenged, like I'm operating at a level I could be.
- I don't like what I'm doing right now. I'd hate to do it for several more years.
- I had professional goals I didn't achieve.
- Those on the "in" get promoted; I never will.
- I had dreams at one time, and I will never accomplish them while in this job.
- It's sucking the life out of me.

Although the final one may seem a little dramatic — for those who are in that situation, it's a reality.

For all of those who participated, actually writing down the things they most feared would happen actually made it easy for them to construct their Failure Scenarios.

One of the Failure Scenarios I received said this:

10 years later, I'm still stuck in this (gosh darn) job that I stopped enjoying 10 years ago. It's stopped being a challenge, and I gave up giving a (darn) a long time ago. Now I just go through the motions, counting the days until I no longer have to put up with this (stuff).

MY FUTURE WILL BE DIFFERENT. I HAVE THE POWER TO ENSURE MY SUCCESS SCENARIO BECOMES MY NEW REALITY. I WILL DO THE FOLLOWING TO MAKE SURE I SUCCEED IN REACHING MY GOAL.

Although I chose to censor the profanity for this book, the fact that it was there showed that he truly felt the emotion associated with his scenario—exactly as it should be.

Another simply wrote for their Failure Scenario,

> With the money I'm making right now, I can't send my kids to college. I won't have any money for retirement. I won't be able to travel like my husband and I want, and I'll have to depend on the government for my health care.
>
> MY FUTURE WILL BE DIFFERENT. I HAVE THE POWER TO ENSURE MY SUCCESS SCENARIO BECOMES MY NEW REALITY. I WILL DO THE FOLLOWING TO MAKE SURE I SUCCEED IN REACHING MY GOAL.

An additional Failure Scenario read,

> I know I can do better! I just never hit my stride and achieved what I believe in my heart I can do! I see people around me hitting these high goals, and I don't think they have anything that I don't have. But they're setting the records, and I feel like I'm standing still.
>
> MY FUTURE WILL BE DIFFERENT. I HAVE THE POWER TO ENSURE MY SUCCESS SCENARIO BECOMES MY NEW REALITY. I WILL DO THE FOLLOWING TO MAKE SURE I SUCCEED IN REACHING MY GOAL.

You may be able to relate to some of the above, as well as coming up with others that have meaning to you directly. I believe — based on many experiences of myself and my clients — that if you truly try, you can manifest some very emotional issues in both your Success and Failure Scenarios. And those emotions, along with your Action Plan, will help ensure that you reach your goals, no matter how lofty they are.

The emotional aspects of both potential success and potential failure are the most important factors of all, and ones that are too frequently ignored. We need to harness the unstoppable power of our emotions, both positive and negative, to help us break through the barriers that could otherwise wear us down and ultimately keep us from reaching and sustaining our long-term goals.

We must visualize twice daily the true emotional ramifications of both success and failure in reaching our goal, and use that emotional energy to propel us forward when other emotions may try to slow us down.

These have been merely a few examples from which you can gain perspective to apply to your own situation, no matter what that is.

In developing your Oxcart, consider these questions:

- What would be a lofty, yet attainable, goal?
- Why do you want to attain that goal?
- What difference will it make in your life?
- What difference will it make in the lives of others?
- What if you don't reach your goal?

Use these answers and more to develop your Success and Failure Scenarios, and make them as strong and emotional as you possibly can.

A final great example of how the Success and Failure Scenarios can drive you in business is my friend Barbara. After 30 years of running her mortgage company, Barbara had hit a plateau. The company's bottom line was constant, but there just wasn't any growth.

She couldn't really blame her employees — she personally seemed to have lost her fire. After all, she had a more-than-comfortable income, was set for her retirement, and didn't have many cares in the world. Why work harder when she didn't have to? She did seem to have an uneasy feeling, though. It was as if her life had lost some of its fire. In some ways, she missed the hard-driving days of building her company, but somehow she didn't have the motivation to do it again.

She decided to attempt The Oxcart Technique, though she had no idea what she could put as her Success and Failure Scenarios. It was her husband who helped her rekindle a dream she'd had many years ago. After hearing a speaker talk about the 1994 Rwandan massacre, she had dreamed about helping him with his quest of building a school to teach the widows and orphans of that massacre some marketable skills, such as sewing and carpentry. These skills would allow them to buy food and other necessities without having to turn to dishonorable means.

Years of toiling at her job erased that dream from Barbara's memory, until it was naught but a distant recollection.

Suddenly, it was a whole different ball game!

After doing the research, Barbara found that she actually could make an impact! Instead of working just to increase her personal bottom line, if she set up a fund of $150,000, she could build the entire school, plus have the crops in place that they could use and sell to be completely self-sustaining in the future.

Now Barbara had a goal and a reason to achieve it— something she could be extremely passionate about.

Her Success and Failure Scenarios were easy: If she achieved her goal, she could change the lives of hundreds, or more, who have endured one of the world's worst atrocities and were fighting every day merely to survive. If she didn't, they had no hope. Now Barbara could get to work with renewed vigor and intensity.

After you've set up your Success and Failure Scenarios, it will be time to develop your Action Plan. As you've learned in this book, your Action Plan is simply those steps that you will need to complete to reach your goal.

How do you know what those are? Research. Brainstorm. Talk to people in your industry who are more successful than you are. Talk to fellow employees, if applicable.

If you're an employee, ask your boss (or whoever does your performance evaluations) what steps you could take to be the best you could possibly be in your position. Then, perhaps, you could ask them what steps you could take to be deemed worthy of a raise or promotion.

I realize that there are as many possible points on a Business Action Plan as stars in the sky. But a common thread I see in many professions is the necessity to network—to get out and meet new people. Even if you're not in a profession that lives and dies on this — such as outside sales, real estate, or investment advising — there are many more professions you may not think of that could benefit from this skill as well.

Most attorneys would like more clients. Many doctors and dentists would like their patient schedule to be even busier and more profitable. Pretty much anyone in the business world would like more people walking through their front doors. And, if you are looking to improve your position in the job or business world, we all understand that "it's who you know."

So how do you make all that happen? Just get out there and network! And, if you have employees who would benefit from doing so, teach them to do the same.

The challenge I've seen is that too few people know how to network well.

They'll go to events, find the people they know and chat with them, then leave and wonder why they're not pulling in more business!

Just as in almost everything, there's a wrong way to do it, and a right way to do it.

The first step to doing it right is to identify every potential networking opportunity in your area, and get them on your schedule.

Ideas include:

- Industry-specific organizations
- Chamber of Commerce
- Networking groups such as Business Network International
- Service organizations like Rotary, Lions Club, and Kiwanis
- Community events
- Business Grand Openings
- Fundraising events

Many organizations will let you visit their club once, free of charge, as part of their recruiting efforts. Focus on the ones that will lead you to the most contacts the quickest, and disregard the rest. Also, don't attend too many at the same time, because, as you'll see, you'll need enough time to follow up with everyone you meet there.

Some helpful hints when going to networking events from those who have attended many events are: Dress slightly above what you perceive the normal dress of the event to be. You want to come across as professional, but not haughty. Next, wear comfortable shoes that will allow you to walk around and meet people.

It's also usually wise to eat prior to the event, so you're not carrying food around and you can put your focus where it needs to be: on meeting people. Finally, whatever you do, don't get drunk, or even tipsy. Few things can make a worse first impression.

Always keep in mind that your goal at these events is to meet as many people as possible, and to get, not just give, as many business cards as possible. It doesn't help if all you do is hand out business cards. Let's face it: Most people either throw them away, or throw them in a drawer. That being said, come armed with plenty of your own business cards, as well. Odds are, you will be asked for them, and it seems very unprofessional to not have them with you.

When I first started networking, I was incredibly nervous. I had no idea what to say! I didn't consider myself an interesting person compared to all of these world-traveling business types. I admit it: I was intimidated.

Then I realized a truth of networking that literally set me free:

> *The art of conversation, much like the art of sales, is not in the things that you say, but rather the questions you ask.*

Have you ever been to a social event and had someone come up to you and keep talking and talking and talking? Then, as soon as you tried to get a word in, they would interrupt and start off on a whole new story? Don't be that person.

On the other hand, have you had someone asking questions of you, showing sincere interest in what you have to say? How did you feel about them? Most likely you felt fantastic. You'd like to spend more time around them.

That's the key.

YOU be interested in THEM.

Be more interested than interesting.

Ask questions, get them talking, and keep them talking.

Something as simple as:

"What do you do for a living?"

"How long have you been doing that?"

"What do you like best about it?"

"What do you like to do for fun?"

"How long have you been doing that?"

"What do you like best about it?" are all good openers.

Then, ask follow-up questions to delve deeper:

"How so?"

"Tell me more about that."

After a short conversation, remembering that you need to meet as many people as you can in the time provided, you can say something like, "I know we need to get around and network, but I'd really like to hear more about this. Can I get your card, and call you up and buy you a cup of coffee sometime?" I have never been turned down on this.

Some networking events actually have everyone pass around their business cards, or simply hand out the contact information of everyone who is in attendance, without necessarily meeting everyone. When an event gives the advantage of automatically having everyone's contact information, it also comes with the disadvantage of not having met everyone.

This challenge can be easily overcome.

First of all, do your best to at least shake hands briefly with as many people as possible at the event.

Then, immediately after the event, you need to call every single person you have a card or contact information for. Please read this very carefully: You can't wait until the next day. They won't remember you at all the next day. You must call them the day of the event.

Your phone call can be as simple as: "Hi, is this Jim? Jim, this is Terry L. Fossum — I met you briefly at the networking event today. Hey, if you don't mind, I'd like to buy you a cup of coffee, find out more about what you do, and tell you more about what I do. I may be able to send you business. Would that be okay?"

In all my years of networking, I've only been turned down once, as they were extremely busy at the time, and they still ended up meeting with me at a later time, when their schedule was more open.

What do you do when you meet them for coffee? You guessed it: Ask questions. Be interested in them.

Find common ground — something you're both interested in, and talk about that.

If they are more of a bottom-line business person, get right down to business, and discuss how you may be able to refer business to each other.

Others may want to chat more, to get to know you better before they feel comfortable sending business your way. The main goal is to establish a relationship.

Remember:

People don't do business with businesses
— they do business with people.

They need to know they can trust you. They need to know you have their best interests in mind—that you're not there merely attempting to take, but to give. Then, and only then, will they do business with you, and perhaps even lead you to others you may do business with, as well.

Use their products or services, if at all possible. Then, if you are satisfied with them, refer people to them. Make recommendations regarding others they may contact. Help them build their business.

Take notes on items you talked about: even simple details about their families, hobbies, and important events. If you ask about these things in future conversations, they'll know you were actually listening, and truly care.

When you take these actions enough times, you'll have more contacts — and more business — than you've ever had before.

Earlier in this chapter, we learned how Barbara got reengaged in her mortgage company due to her renewed passion for helping the widows and orphans of Rwanda. Her next step was to develop an Action Plan that could make her Success Scenario a reality.

Here is the initial plan she set up for herself:

- Join the National Association of Realtors, attend every meeting possible, and network.
- Join the Association of Mortgage Lenders, attend every meeting possible, and network.
- Follow up with every new contact the same day I meet them, to set up a coffee meeting.
- Contact 2 Realtors, investment advisors, or insurance agents every day, to set up a coffee meeting.
- Send out 5 hand-written cards each week to people I met with.
- Write at least 2 applications each week.
- Contact each buyer/listing agent/selling agent of current deals every Tuesday.
- Help my team members set their Oxcart and monitor them daily.

Her next step was to stimulate her employees to excel. Understanding that the pace of the pack is determined by the pace of the leader, she immediately posted her Oxcart and began taking her daily actions. Her staff saw her newfound enthusiasm. They noticed the actions she was taking. They began to feel her excitement.

Now it was time to help focus them on what was truly important to them, and become the most powerful they could possibly be. That's exactly what we'll discuss in the chapter on Setting Your Team on Fire.

For now, it's time to get to work.

The great quarterback Roger Staubach once said,

> *"Spectacular achievements are always preceded*
> *by unspectacular preparation."*

Develop your Success and Failure Scenarios and your Action Plan, post them where you will read them out loud twice a day, and expect even more enormous success than perhaps even you thought possible.

With enough passion, anything is possible!

SELF-EXAMINATION QUESTION: Out of top nine important aspects of your job/business listed in this chapter, what are the most important ones to you? How would you answer the question 'What are the things you most fear about being stuck in the same job that you don't like, for whatever reason, for a long period of time?' What would be your ultimate job, position, or business?

CHAPTER 14

Blow the Roof Off of Your Sales

"Life is a matter of choices, and every choice you make makes you."

— John C. Maxwell

In the first edition of this book, I wrote the chapter on 'Taking Your Job, Professional, or Business to New Heights', and figured that would cover the sales professions. But after it was so quickly and widely adopted by sales professionals around the world, hit #1 on Wall Street Journal, lauded by some of the top minds in business, talked about on major podcasts and shows, and on and on, that I decided to dedicate a separate chapter in the second edition just for all of us who are helping people find the products and services they need most – the sales professionals!

What I'm about to teach you is EXACTLY how I went from failing, and failing and failing for YEARS in business, to become part of the fraction of 1% in my entire industry – in the world.

You ready?

Let's see if you can relate to this:

You started into a sales position, and you were really excited - and maybe scared as heck.

But you loved the possibilities and the money you could make doing it, and hopefully found a product or service you can believe in, and feel good putting your name, conscience, and reputation behind.

You've gone through sales training, maybe even learned the exact steps you need to take every day to succeed. You know it works – some of the top people in your industry have made a TON of dough doing it, but it just hasn't worked for you! At least not to level you want it too.

And you've tried, and you've tried! But you just don't seem to be able to get traction, no matter how hard you try!

And now, you may be starting to question if you can actually do this. Life may be getting in the way, I mean, you have a lot of priorities in your life! People and things that are important to you! And there just doesn't seem to be enough time in the day to get everything done.

You may even be at a crossroads. Should I continue doing this – or find myself a 'real' job.

Here's something to know: You're not alone.

In fact, on a national average, 73% of sales reps fail. 73%! And there's a reason why.

The Problem:

As you well know, as salespeople, we have to get out of our comfort zone; we have to do things we don't really want to do, so we hesitate!

Things like:

- We don't like to feel like we're 'selling' people. It feels icky to us!
- We don't look forward to customers being rude or distrustful of them
- We get tired of overcoming objections – it feels like a constant battle to us.
- We don't like making new contacts
- We have trouble picking up the 1000 lb phone
- We hate cold calls
- Afraid we'll say the wrong thing
- Afraid we won't know the answer

- We avoid going to networking events
- Even going up to people and talking to them is uncomfortable
- So instead we focusing on trying to close the few prospects we have and we don't get new ones.
- Often, we don't even follow up with the contacts they've made – hey, we might get a no!

These things are out of our comfort zone, and it's scary out there! It's painful out there! I feel safe in my comfort zone. But the problem is: the comfort zone is where dreams go to die.

The question has always been, how do we get out of our comfort zone, and doing the things we KNOW they need to do?

What we've done to motivate ourselves:

Traditionally, we learned we should visualize great positive outcomes, something to work toward. So we focus on how much money we can make, and what that will do for us. We get fired up at sales meetings and competitions and awards.

We learned to write down our goals, because the Harvard goalsetting story showed that 100% of the people who wrote down their goals reached them.

And still, about 73% of salespeople fail.

Why is that?

In this chapter, I'm going to repeat some of the things previously written in the book for two reasons:

1. They bear repeating so they're fresh on your mind.
2. I know salespeople: Half of you skipped the first chapters and went right to this one!

So, first of all, let's get rid of the Harvard Goal study. Why? Because it never happened. That's right – it's been written up in books, used countless time in presentations, but it never actually happened. Someone made it up. Harvard has confirmed it, along with Yale, and everyone else it's been attributed to. That's not to say writing down your goals isn't important. It's critical! But having a goal without the motivation behind it is useless.

Now, on to the positive visualizations, something to work toward. Also very important, but not enough, or more people would reach their goals!

So, why isn't it enough?

Prospect Theory, which won the Nobel Prize when applied to economics, taught us that often a negatively framed message is more powerful than a positively framed message. In other words, we'll often work harder to get away from something than we will to go toward something.

Here's the problem: We equate getting out of our comfort zone with the pain of the 'stick' – something we want to stay away from. It's painful. We don't like it. So that overrides our wanting to go toward the carrot, or the positive visualization, or success in their field.

There's our disconnect! For most of us, we don't move forward because the pain of getting out of our comfort zone is greater than the pleasure of the dream, so we make excuses, have terrible time management, don't follow up, life gets in the way – everything that keeps us away from the pain of the stick!

What's the solution?

The Oxcart Technique integrates both the carrot and the stick to motivate your teams to take the appropriate actions every single day.

How?

It's a simple, but extremely effective, 3-page technique you create for yourself and read out loud every single day.

The first page is you Failure Scenario.

THE FAILURE SCENARIO

The Failure Scenario provides a visualization that's more painful than getting out of your comfort zone. Its sole purpose is to create enough emotion to make you want to get out of that comfort zone and take action.

We start with the question: What happens if you fail at your job?

We could simply say 'I'll get fired', but that isn't enough. Getting fired is a fact, not an emotion; and emotion, not fact, is the driver of all action. If you want more action, you create more emotion.

So we ask the question 'What does getting fired REALLY look like?'

Things like:

- What will that failure feel like? How will your loved ones feel about that? Will they be disappointed? Who all are you letting down if you fail here?
- What will it feel like to have to look for another job, when you just failed at this one? How big of a pain will that be? What will you do for employment? What will your next job be – if there is one?
- What about you bills? How will you pay their mortgage or car payment? What about supporting your family? What could happen if you can't pay your bills?

If you truly internalize this, it should be incredibly painful. And, the main point: more painful than getting out of your comfort zone.

It will have your subconsciousness crying out 'I'll do whatever I need to do to make sure that never happens!' And what is 'whatever I need to'? Getting out of your comfort zone and accomplishing the 2nd page: The Action Plan.

THE ACTION PLAN

The Action Plan is the daily actions you know you need to take to be successful. This will almost certainly come from your sales trainers and coaches, but feel free to also learn from some of the most successful people in your office. What do THEY do? What are their tricks of the trade? If you want to BE the best, learn from the best! How many new contacts will you make each day? How many follow ups? What are other ways you can reach new prospects? How many minutes per day on advanced learning, or other ways to improve your closing rate?

After you've just read your Failure Scenario, if you've done it right, you can't wait to do the actions on your plan so you can get away from the stick, your

Failure Scenario, and to the third page, your Success Scenario: How amazing life will be when you take those daily actions?

The Success Scenario

What does success in your industry look like? Not just moderate success – REAL success? And again, the answer can't just be 'money', because money is a fact – not an emotion. You need to create emotion. More emotion = more action.

- What can that money buy? The ability to buy a home to raise a family? To be able to send the kids to college if they want to? If travel, then with who, and what will that FEEL like?
- Can you get into a management position that doesn't require you personally to hit sales quotas every month? What does that mean? Peace of mind? More stability for family?
- How will you feel about yourself? Will you be proud? Feel like you've accomplished something?
- Who else will be proud of you? Your spouse, your kids, your parents, your friends?

Just as in the Failure Scenario, it's critical to build as much emotion as possible into this.

Each morning before work, and each afternoon after work, you read all the pages in this order:

- The Failure Scenario to create pain and the need to take action to get away from it
- The Action Plan to give a clear path away from that pain, and toward pleasure
- The Success Scenario to give your subconscious the pleasure of having taken the actions to avoid pain, and gain the pleasure that comes with being a highly successful member of the team

Every time you read the 3 pages, it should be like going through an emotional journey, from sad to happy, as you internalize that either the Failure or Success Scenarios will be your future, and the choice is in your complete control, depending on whether or not you've taken the action in your Action Plan every day.

It's this emotional journey that compels you to take the actions that you WANT to take each day – actions that will lead to your success, and propels you to reaching goals you never have before.

Let's look at a couple of examples to help you in creating your own.

The first one is from Chris, an extremely nice young man in his early 30s who made some bad decisions early on that landed him in prison. Since then he's served his time, and is working hard in his sales job to improve his life every day; and the lives of those close to him!

His Failure Scenario reads:

Failure Scenario

I had a plan to simplify the buying process and make a team that excels at following the process that we developed but I failed. I didn't put the time or effort into making this come to fruition. My staff has lost faith in my ability to lead. My boss no longer trusts me to get the job done and hovers over me to make sure I don't screw things up. All the pressure from my failure causes resentment and a poor attitude. They bring in another person to do what I could not. Their hard work proves that I am no longer needed, and I lose my job and the stability and sense of accomplishment that made me love what I did.

I see others succeeding without me while I try to find work just to make ends meet. My girlfriend leaves me because my bad attitude proves to be too difficult to be around and it makes her look bad to be around me. I fall back on bar tending which puts me in the same bad crowd that I have tried so hard to avoid. I can't afford the house I bought so that I can be close to my dad as he ages. I must work late hours and often just to have a fraction of the stability that I had before. I spent what little money I do have on drugs and alcohol just so I can feel a glimmer of the happiness I have already had without it once before. I can no longer take time to see my family or travel. I lose my ability to invest in my future.

My mom and dad eventually pass away wondering if I will ever make something out of myself. Instead of being there for them in the final days I shy away, embarrassed of who I became. I never hear the words "I'm proud" ever again. They are disappointed in my failures and unrealized potential. They die wondering where I am and why I wasn't there. I must live with this the rest of my miserable life.

As a last-ditch effort, I turn to criminal activity to make easy money because I don't want to work for what I have. I eventually get busted again and end up where I was all those years ago. With a record that won't go away this time I have even more trouble finding work or someone willing to give me a chance. I work odd jobs and never set anything aside for retirement. My health suffers from the abuse I put myself through. I have no insurance, so I am riddled with debt and constantly struggling.

I have ruined my relationships with my friends and family and end up alone… Bitter and full of anger at myself for failing all those years ago. My legacy is not one of success but one of laziness and poor decisions. People use me as an example as how not to live life instead of looking up to me. I am what people though I would be all those years ago. A failure. I eventually die alone and angry surrounded by failures and regret. I can't think of a worse way to go…

MY FUTURE WILL BE DIFFERENT. I HAVE THE POWER TO ENSURE MY SUCCESS SCENARIO BECOMES MY NEW REALITY. I WILL DO THE FOLLOWING TO ENSURE I SUCCEED IN REACHING MY GOAL.

This is a Failure Scenario that's getting him past his own self-doubts and excuses every single day, and pushing him out of that comfort zone that's held him back in the past; way out in his case! And it's leading him toward his Success Scenario every single day:

Success Scenario

I have excelled in my industry. I manage a team that looks up to me. We have created a process that is simple and effective. Our closing rates are the best in the business and our customers are happy and eager to come back again. My team is making great money and so am I. We all love to come to work every day. I get to see people succeed in ways they didn't think was possible. I get to help people change their lives and the lives of their loved ones.

My success has allowed me to create a future that I am proud of and that my parents will be proud of. I can be close to them and spend time with them as they age. I get to repay them for all the help they have given me over the years. I am able to put aside money to ensure that I can retire wealthy and comfortable. My legacy is one of success and kindness. People see me as someone to aspire to be like. I become other people's mentor and guide them to their own success. My new relationship blossoms into love and eventually a family that I can take care of. I get to share my success and pass down my good habits to my children so that they too can be successful in whatever they choose to do.

I can retire while I'm still energetic and eager to explore. We are able to travel and create memories with each other. I grow old knowing that I did everything I could in life and didn't waste any more time. I get to look back at my life in my final days and smile while I'm surrounded by loved ones that respect me and have found their own success with my help. I can't think of a better way to go!

THIS IS MY FUTURE. I WILL DO WHATEVER IT TAKES TO MAKE THIS HAPPEN. TODAY, I WILL TAKE THE ACTIONS IN MY PLAN SO I MAY ENJOY THE HAPPINESS I DESERVE.

I'm happy to give the update that Chris' Success Scenario is coming true! He has been promoted to Sales Manager, has gotten national company recognition, and now has a new child who he is proving for and setting a great example for every single day.

Sienna didn't go to prison, but her history is full of its own challenges. After making several bad decisions, spending far past her income, running up massive credit card debt, and borrowing money from friends, family, and anyone else who would listen, she declared bankruptcy.

It was time to turn her life around completely.

She may not have had a great educational background, but she did have two things going for her: she has a great personality, and she's not afraid of hard work. So she decided to give auto sales a try. It didn't go well. As you can imagine, auto sales is a very hard business, with a tremendous failure rate, and before long, management was ready to let her go.

That is, all of management except one of them. One of her bosses saw something in her the others didn't; he believed in her; and that's often all some of us need. Add to that, he had read the first edition of this book and was using it for himself! He shared it with her, and here's her Failure and Success Scenarios:

My Failure Scenario

I've already hit my failure scenario once. Two years ago, I filed for bankruptcy. Declared to everyone that I was in debt and could not pay my bills. I had collections upon collections and was months behind on rent. I couldn't even afford to pay any of my bills and had to rely on the state to step in and help me.

I was ruining my relationship with my family because I was constantly asking to borrow money without a promise of when I would be able to pay it back. I even ended up borrowing some from my friends and it took me forever to pay them back. I'm still working on paying my grandparents back. I now also have a stain on my credit report. One that I will be stuck with for the next 6 years. Now, every time I try to go get a loan from a bank or a credit card, the first thing they see is that Bankruptcy. Not that I make all my payments on time now or that I make more than enough money to pay the loan. They see that at one point, I got so behind on bills that I had to declare bankruptcy and now weigh the risk of giving me a loan. Is this guy going to be able to pay us back this time? Or is he going to declare bankruptcy again and will we not be paid back? Most of the time it's not even a real person that decides my fate. The computer sees bankruptcy and automatically declines it before any real person has the chance to look at it. I never want to be in that position again. IF I ever got to that position, I would lose my house, my truck, I'm sure Emory would consider leaving me and the depression could get so bad that I may even lose my job. My family could start thinking that "that's all she'll ever amount to".

MY FUTURE WILL BE DIFERENT! I HAVE THE POWER TO ASSURE MY SUCCESS SCENARIO BECOMES MY NEW REALITY! I WILL DO THE FOLLOWING TO INSURE I SUCCEED IN REACHING MY GOAL!

She worked with her supervisor on her Action Plan, and has been sticking with it so her Success Scenario could be her new future!

My Success Scenario

This is where I want to be. I will keep perfecting my skills and knowledge to the point where I will rise to the top of not only this dealership, but the family of dealerships. I will become one of the most well-known car salesman in the state and will be recognized at (national car company name) events as exceeding and going above all expectations. I will become a poster child for the company and the example for how all customers are expected to be treated when they walk through our doors. And eventually, I'll move into a management position where I will be able to train everyone below me to exude the same kind of professional behavior that I do. That people want to come here because they have heard of the amazing experience that people received here. That my original customers will feel comfortable and trust any salesperson under me because they trust me.

With this all, I know I will make a lot more money than I am and with it I will become financially free. My family will have the house of their dreams and it will be paid for. We will drive the vehicles we WANT, not the vehicles we settled for. We will have a lake cabin dubbed the "Summer Funzone" where all of our friends, family and kids friends will want to come and spend the weekend. We will take some amazing vacations and go places we've always wanted to go without having to ever worry about "If we can afford it" or without having to limit what we do because we don't have enough money to do it. I'll take my grandpa on hunts that he would never have imagined going on and send my mom on the vacations of her dreams. I'll be able to help my grandparents have the retirement they've always dreamt of. My family will never have to worry about "IF we can pay the bills", in fact, they won't even worry about the bills at all because we won't even know that they are coming out of the bank accounts because there is more than enough money in them. I will be able to give my kids the best graduation present ever, by telling them that if they so choose, their college education will be fully paid for and they won't have to worry about money at all during their college career. That they will be able to fully focus on school and having fun because "Mom and Dad got them covered". For myself, I'll be able to get the country club memberships I've always wanted without feeling guilty for getting them. I'll be able to go play some amazing and once in a lifetime courses with some of my closest friends and them not have to worry about paying for anything. My family will be the happiest ever and it will be because they don't have to live with the burden/fear of not having enough money for all of life's adventures.

THIS IS MY FUTURE. I WILL DO WHATEVER IT TAKES TO MAKE THIS HAPPEN. TODAY, I WILL TAKE THE ACTIONS IN MY PLAN SO I MAY ENJOY THE HAPPINESS I DESERVE.

Not only did Sienna make salesperson of the month for her dealership, but was recognized nationally with the prestigious Mark of Excellence Award from her international company!

When developing your own Oxcart, it's very important that you are developing your Failure and Success Scenarios on your own. It's YOUR words, not any supervisors. It's not them kicking you in the butt to get it done – you're kicking yourself in the butt! And let's face it: That's the only way we're truly going to get motivated. It has to come from ourselves. WE have to be truly inspired to take the actions – and that's what the Oxcart Technique is all about. Focusing our energy using both the power of the carrot and the stick to take the actions we really need to take – that we WANT to take, but sometimes need that extra push to do it.

Right along those lines, if you are a supervisor or business owner who wants to implement the Oxcart Technique with your teams, this is critical: you cannot force this upon them! Each individual has to choose on their own to use the Oxcart Technique, or it almost certainly won't work. Just like their 'stick' has to be of their own creation, even the choice to use 'the stick' must be as well!

They have to learn what the technique is, and then make their own decision that they truly want to reach new, higher goals, and are willing to do what it takes to do so.

In fact, I highly recommend contacting one of my team to help you implement the Oxcart Technique in your company, to make sure you get the maximum effectiveness. They're trained on the subtle nuances that will make all the difference in the world in helping you lead your team to levels you may never have even dreamed of before! And just imagine what that will do for your bottom line!

So you if or your teams are ready to bust out of your comfort zone, get past the fears, self-doubts, and excuses, and create your own amazing future, you know what to do: use both the power of the carrot and the stick, and start making it happen!

At the end: SELF-EXAMINATION QUESTION: After reading this chapter and the chapter on Excuses, what do you honestly feel has held you back from reaching your goals in the past? Is avoiding your Failure Scenario and living your Success Scenario enough to get you past these in the future?

CHAPTER 15

Network Marketing Done Right

"Network marketing done right can be a dream come true. Network marketing done wrong is a nightmare. Do it right and live the dream!"

— Terry l. Fossum

Network marketing often gets a bad rap, but no matter what the naysayers impart, network marketing is a booming industry. In 2022, the global MLM market was valued at $201 billion, and by the end of 2030 it's predicted to exceed a whopping $329 billion. The CAGR, or Compound Annual Growth Rate, is predicted to be a whopping 6.5% between 2023 and 2030, putting it considerably above many other industries.

In a 2022 survey by the Direct Selling Association, 89% of MLM participants reported being satisfied or extremely satisfied with their involvement in the sector. That satisfaction comes not just in the form of financial success, but also in the new friendships and experiences that come from the industry, and the immense personal growth that occurs in most every person who puts in any effort at all. In my opinion, there is no better personal growth experience in the world than active participation in a reputable network marketing company.

Why do I feel this way? Because I know what it did for me. This is a chapter that is near and dear to me, as I was Blessed to reach the top 1% of the entire industry in the world. When I did, I enjoyed everything we've heard about: the amazing recurring income, being able to help people achieve their dreams that I had never even met before, go on crazy adventures all around the world, make amazing friends around the world, have the opportunity to make a difference in the world through my philanthropic efforts, go on amazing success trips, and most important of all to me: when I married into three teenage and preteen boys, I was able to retire so I could focus entirely on raising them, and still have a recurring income stream.

In fact, during that period of time, I became the Scoutmaster for the two youngest ones, and help them become Eagle Scouts. That even led me to be chosen to represent all of Boy Scouts of America on a survival reality show, as the oldest contestant on the entire show, pitting against special forces guys, military survival instructors, and much more. Knowing I would be the underdog and not wanting to embarrass the entire Boy Scouts of America, the income and free time allowed me to travel into the Amazon Jungle to prepare for the show, and meet with experts across the country to hone up on my skills. The result: the fat, old Scoutmaster won the show!

The truth is, everything you've heard about the industry CAN come true. It can lead to an absolutely amazing lifestyle that most people can only dream of. I'm living proof!

The bad news: For many of the people who join the industry, it never happens.

The good news: we've identified why.

I will FULLY admit that for me, it almost didn't. I wasn't one of those instant success stories you hear people talk about; those people who come on board, and within just a few months build this huge organization, and win all of the contests, and that people use as an example about how quickly you can turn your life around.

Quite the opposite. I struggled, and struggled, and struggled. For YEARS, I struggled. I watch these people on stage who came on board with my company way after I did, and had so much more success than me.

And I went to all the conferences, and I'd get all excited! I listened to the calls every week, and I read of all of the mind set books, and wrote down my goals, and did the mantras, and visualizations, and dream boards; but nothing seemed to work for me. It just didn't keep me on track doing what I was supposed to do every day. And the excuses seemed to make sense, and life got in the way, and my fears of rejection rose higher, as did my self-doubts as the months and years went by, and I still wasn't reaching my goals.

But I tried, and failed, and I tried, and failed, and I tried, and tried and tried. Until I reached a point where I just couldn't try any more.

And I gave up.

See, I don't just write about all of this stuff. I actually went through it myself. The entire Oxcart Technique and everything behind is born from actual experience. Actual failure. Actual pain.

Keeping in mind my story that when I was growing up, one of our neighbors told my father "Not a single one of your boys will never grow up to be anything", when I finally didn't have it in me to fail any more, I walked into the bathroom, looked at myself in the mirror, and told myself "I guess he was right. You really never are going to grow up to be anything."

Take a moment and picture that for a minute. Picture the look in my eyes. Picture the tears; the sadness; the devastation. Everyone reads about all the successes at this point in my life, but no one was there in the bathroom as I finally gave up.

But at that low moment, something happened. Something clicked inside of me. Quite frankly, I got pissed off. "No!" I said to myself. "For the sake of the memory of my dad if nothing else, I refuse to let that son-of-a-bitch be right!" (pardon the profanity, but I'm being real here). And that did it. I got back up, brushed myself off, and got back at it again. But I did it from a different perspective! Not from some pie-in-the-sky, positive visualization or mantra. Those things got me excited and made me feel happy, but didn't keep me out of my comfort zone actually doing the things I needed to do to make them come true.

Now I understand why none of those things worked for me, just as they don't work for most people!

First of all, I never believed that something like that would happen to a guy like me! I'm not one of the special people, the 'beautiful people'! Next, I don't care about big houses, or fancy cars, or anything like that – that's someone else's dream. I'm my happiest in a tent! And finally, after understanding Prospect Theory, I understand that I, just like everyone else in the world, will do more to avoid pain that go toward pleasure, so even if I did find a positive visualization that I cared about and believed would happen to a guy like me, it still wouldn't be enough to get me through the pain of getting out of my comfort zone!

So now when I hit all the "no's" and "It's a pyramid scheme" and "Stop trying to sell me something", or my team members quitting, or my sponsors quitting, or product or company changes, and all the other setbacks, I didn't care! Maybe all of those things stopped me in the past as I was trying to go toward this positive visualization like I was taught, but NOTHING would get in the way of proving that son-of-a-(gun) wrong! I had something pushing me forward; pushing me past all of the fears, self-doubts, and excuses. Something much more powerful than any positive visualization could ever be.

And the Oxcart Technique was born.

It was then that I realized that the carrot, the positive visualization wasn't enough to pull me out of my comfort zone, but the stick, the negative effects of not taking the actions PUSHED me out of my comfort zone, and got me into action.

So I wrote out something I called a 'Failure Scenario', just like you've been reading about in this book, and wrote out a complete Success Scenario that was important to me, then I wrote my daily actions that I would absolutely take come heck or high water, posted them up just like you've read in this book, and got into action. Long term action.

The results were amazing.

I actually started reaching my goals, and moving up the ladder. As I did, people started asking me what I was doing, so I taught them. Before I knew it, I had rooms full of people listening to me! I became one of those success stories!

Don't get me wrong: I still had challenges and setbacks, but I was better able to push through them, because I had the power of the Oxcart Technique.

Some of my favorite coaching that I do is with people in this industry who are serious about reaching their goals, because I've been there and done that. I've gotten the cuts and bruises; the setbacks and disappointments. I understand the challenges and the emotions that go with them.

I understand how difficult it is for most people to do the things that are completely uncomfortable, such as prospecting, following up, and overcoming objections, necessary to build a large organization around the globe.

Much of this is covered in the previous chapter on Sales, so if you skipped that one, please go back and read it. But I wanted to give you some industry-specific examples of Success and Failure Scenarios to draw from, so gave network marketing its own chapter. For your Action Plan, use the materials your organization, company, or Senior Partners are teaching.

As you've learned from this book, the biggest challenge people have is getting and staying out of their comfort zones; and the answer to that is to build a Failure Scenario that is much more uncomfortable than your fears, self-doubts, and excuses. If you've done this correctly, the internalization of your Failure Scenario and the emotion that it produces will drive you out of your comfort zone.

Again, Prospect Theory taught us that we'll do more to avoid pain than to go toward pleasure, which is why positive visualizations such as dream boards, mantras, and manifestations aren't enough to get people through the pain of getting out of their comfort zones and taking the actions they need to take each day to succeed in this industry. Thus the high failure rate in the industry.

If you truly want to be successful, you need to do what the masses aren't doing: don't just rely on the 'carrot' (the Success Scenario, or positive visualization), but incorporate the much more powerful element of the 'stick' (the Failure Scenario).

Remember: the 'why do I HAVE to is much more powerful than the 'why do I WANT to', and will keep you going when the uncomfortable fears, self-doubts, and excuses start to slow you down, or threaten to stop you all together.

Let's look at some examples:

Joanne, one of my coaching clients, was kind enough to share her Oxcart Technique with us. Joanne is a strong, independent community leader who controls a room just by walking into it. This leadership has rubbed off on her quickly growing organization where she's teaching men and women both to take control of their lives and chart their own course.

Here's her scenarios:

Failure Scenario: Living Without Financial
Freedom and Personal Autonomy

The pain of failure is tangible and, for me, far more motivating than any vision of success. In my failure scenario, I am financially dependent on others—whether that's my husband, a traditional job, or uncontrollable factors beyond my reach. This dependency would mean that my financial stability is fragile and uncertain, tied to external factors that could change at any moment. It's a life where I'm forced to be a passive observer rather than the active driver of my journey. This lack of control over my future feels hopeless, trapping me in a life dictated by circumstances I can't influence. I know the depths of depression that come with feeling powerless, with seeing no light at the end of the tunnel and no way forward that I control.

If my life and security relied on income that might vanish tomorrow, I would feel like my very purpose was slipping away. Without a means to support myself independently, I would be limited in how I could contribute to the world and help others find a path to growth and freedom. The ultimate failure for me is living without the ability to chart my own course, and without the opportunity to give back in meaningful ways. I know that life as a passenger in my own story is not an option, and it's this vision of failure that drives me to push forward every day.

MY FUTURE WILL BE DIFFERENT. I HAVE THE POWER TO ENSURE MY SUCCESS SCENARIO BECOMES MY NEW REALITY. I WILL DO THE FOLLOWING TO MAKE SURE I SUCCEED IN REACHING MY GOAL.

Success Scenario: Financial Independence and Empowerment of Others

In my success scenario, I am financially stable and independent, with no limitations on my income. I am no longer reliant on external sources or anyone else for my security, and I'm free to chart my own path. My life is driven by purpose and passion, where I am able to use my time and resources to make a meaningful difference in others' lives. I'm empowered not just to support myself but to extend that support to those around me, particularly women who seek growth and freedom.

I envision myself as an example of what is possible—a living proof that professional success and financial freedom can be achieved and maintained by working on one's inner self. Through my journey, I can show others that growth, happiness, and financial independence are within reach, regardless of age or location. My success is more than financial; it's about the ability to use my story to uplift others, speaking success and healing into the lives of those who need it most.

With this success, I have the flexibility and resources to invest in others' growth, fostering change and inspiring hope. My goal is to help people recognize that personal growth is the foundation of professional success, and by pursuing this path, they too can create a life of freedom and purpose. In this scenario, I have the freedom to focus on what truly matters to me: helping others build better lives, creating impact, and being a positive force in the world. This is the life I am working to achieve, one that brings good not only to myself and my family but to people around the world.

THIS IS MY FUTURE. I WILL DO WHATEVER IT TAKES TO MAKE THIS HAPPEN. TODAY, I WILL TAKE THE ACTIONS IN MY PLAN SO I MAY ENJOY THE HAPPINESS I DESERVE.

Todd, another client, envisions a life where he makes a significant difference in the world for causes that are important to him. His greatest fear is living a life of insignificance.

Failure Scenario

I let my fears hold me back, and my self-doubts became my reality because I let them control me, and shape my future. And as a result, I was never able to truly make a mark on the world. I'm actually mad at myself because I bought off on my own excuses. I let things get in the way because I 'didn't have time' – when I know the truth is that I didn't follow my plan because I was afraid. I was afraid people would look down on me for being part of this industry, even though I know that what I offer is far better than their j.o.b.. I felt they were rejecting me personally, instead of rejecting what I was offering them – and I know better! The embarrassment I thought I felt then is far less than the actual embarrassment, and sorry, I feel now.

My dream that not a single animal would die in a shelter ever again never came true. The animals I wanted to save died scared and alone in shelters across the country, not feeling the love they so wanted to share with others. It breaks my heart to think of them.

If I'd only gotten over myself, and thought more about them than I did about myself, maybe things would have turned out different.

MY FUTURE WILL BE DIFFERENT. I HAVE THE POWER TO ENSURE MY SUCCESS SCENARIO BECOMES MY NEW REALITY. I WILL DO THE FOLLOWING TO MAKE SURE I SUCCEED IN REACHING MY GOAL.

Success Scenario

Every day I grew more and more confident in myself and what I can ac-complish. I became a stronger person, and as result, I reached the top of my company. As I'm walking across the stage, I'm not only proud for who I have become, but what I've been able to do with the time and money I now have.

My dream of funding no-kill animal shelters across the country is becoming a reality. My spade or neuter campaign has taken off, as is my Love An Animal For Life program. Because I crashed through all of my fears, and self-doubts, and excuses, and naysayers, and 'no's' and everything else that tried to slow me down or make me stop, I'm a totally different person.

I'm someone who climbed the mountain, and has the scars, and muscle, and confidence, to prove it. And now I know that animals across the country are getting the love they so deserve throughout their lives; and when their life ends, it will be in the loving arms of someone who truly cares about them.

My life means something. The world truly is a better place because I was in it, and I persevered.

THIS IS MY FUTURE. I WILL DO WHATEVER IT TAKES TO MAKE THIS HAPPEN. TODAY, I WILL TAKE THE ACTIONS IN MY PLAN SO I MAY ENJOY THE HAPPINESS I DESERVE.

I actually teared up reading that one. The next one is very powerful as well:

Bobbi is a single mom with three beautiful children, two of who are special needs. Not surprisingly, her main concern wasn't for herself, but for her three children.

Failure Scenario

I didn't do it. My upline told me exactly what I needed to do to succeed. I went to the trainings, I went to the conventions, I believed in the company, I believed in the products, but I guess I just didn't believe in myself. Working two jobs like I've had to do to take care of Paul and Sofie, I didn't have time for Jake, and he kept going down the road that was my biggest fear. But I just didn't have time to give him the attention he needed when the others, and my jobs, took so much.

If I have only stuck to my plan. But now his occasional bouts with the law have turned much more serious, and the drugs he promised he'd never do again gained complete control over him. And the other two; well, I just can't support them forever. What will they do when I'm gone? I've failed them, and I've failed myself.

MY FUTURE WILL BE DIFFERENT. I HAVE THE POWER TO ENSURE MY SUCCESS SCENARIO BECOMES MY NEW REALITY. I WILL DO THE FOLLOWING TO MAKE SURE I SUCCEED IN REACHING MY GOAL.

Wow – that was eye-opening. In fact, painful to read. And that pain is much harder than the pain of getting out of her comfort zone. I would think that would be enough to propel any mother – or father for that matter – to stick to their daily actions no matter what tries to get in the way! And that's the power of the Oxcart Technique.

Happily she follows it up with her Success Scenario, and I'm happy to say that her Success Scenario is slowly-but-steadily coming true.

Success Scenario

It wasn't easy. In fact, it was hard. But it was worth it. I couldn't climb as fast as others, but I climbed. Instead of saying 'it's not the right time', I realized that the only 'right time' is right now. And I stuck to the plan my upline and I developed every single day. I stayed accountable, and didn't make excuses. And all the rejection and disappointment stung at first, but not nearly as bad as that Failure Scenario I wrote, so I ignored them and pressed on.

Now I'm able to spend the time I need to with Jake, and it shows. I can afford to get him into a special school that actually challenges him, so he's not so bored and doesn't get into trouble. In fact, he's found a hobby he loves, and is focused on his studies that are getting him closer to his goal of turning that into a profession. He has a goal!!! He doesn't find his thrills by getting into trouble any more. And Paul and Sofie and in special programs too that are developing them also! They're actually working toward having jobs. They don't have to; I'm putting away a fund to take care of both of them for the rest of their lives. But now they can feel useful and a part of society.

I can't tell you how much success in (this company) means to me, and to my family. It's changed all of my future generations, and I feel really, really good about myself, too. I'm proud. And I haven't felt like that for a long, long time.

THIS IS MY FUTURE. I WILL DO WHATEVER IT TAKES TO MAKE THIS HAPPEN. TODAY, I WILL TAKE THE ACTIONS IN MY PLAN SO I MAY ENJOY THE HAPPINESS I DESERVE.

So what would Failure and Success Scenarios be for you? Remember, emotion, not fact, is the driver of all action, so you have to be as specific, and emotional, as possible. How will it affect you? How will it affect those close to you? What's the worst-case scenario? How does that make you FEEL?

I recently worked with a client whose Failure Scenario included living in her car in her 'golden years'. She was barely holding back tears as she was describing it to me, because it was a very real possibility! But now that she's working with the Oxcart Technique, it has a very low probability of happening, because she is laser focused in to sticking to her daily Action Plan and making sure it never comes true. Instead of that possibility bringing her down, she's using the emotion of it to fire herself up, with a look in her eyes that I haven't seen in a very, very long time. And as she put it, "I finally have hope."

Your Action Plan should be easy: your company has a training program that outlines what your daily activities should be. The important part for you is to make sure it's a plan that you can do, and that you're willing to do, every single day. You can't let someone else dictate your goals for you; they have to be your goals. If they're goals you came up with personally, then you'll be excited to do them each day. If they're goals someone else thrust upon you (even with good intentions), then you won't be excited to reach them, and you may even subconsciously rebel against them!

When you write out your Action Plan, make sure you feel good about every point you're writing. There can't be hesitancy or fear about them, or there's no way you'll stick to them over the long run.

Next, what would a Success Scenario be for you? It's very important that your Success Scenario is your Success Scenario! What is truly important to you? What will make you get up in the morning and want to make those phone calls, do those follow ups, and do everything you know you're suppose to do, but hesitate doing?

If big houses and fancy cars aren't important to you like they weren't for me, don't put there in there! It has to be all about creating and visualizing your dream life, not someone else's. If your dream life is living in a shack in the mountains where you never see anyone else again, put in in there! If it's saving the lives of children or animals, or creating a cure for a disease that's affected the life of someone you know, put it in there! Or, if it is, indeed, staying in 5 star resorts on the beaches of the world while traveling there on your yacht, then, by all means, write it down!

After you have your three pages written out, post them in the order you've learned from this book: Failure Scenario, Action Plan, and Success Scenario, then read them every single day, morning and evening.

I do very much recommend having an accountability partner or team who is also doing the Oxcart Technique that you're speaking with every day to keep each other on track. But be cautioned: If your accountability partner isn't sticking to their goals, get a new accountability partner. If they start believing their own excuses, you may begin believing in your own as well. Run with a pack that is running your speed or more quickly. Those running more slowly than you have the high potential of dragging you down with them. And if you've written your Failure and Success Scenarios well, that is just, plain unacceptable.

Finally, if you want an organization that is laser-focused on their goals, and can fight through all the rejections, fears, self-doubts, excuses, and everything else that holds people back from success, do them the favor of pointing them to the Oxcart Technique as well. They deserve to have every advantage possible in making a difference in their lives, their family's lives, and the causes that are important to them.

I began this chapter saying "Network marketing done right can be a dream come true. Network marketing done wrong is a nightmare." I can say this with full confidence, because I've experienced both.

I fully believe that if you've found a great company with a great product and service you believe in, your Success Scenario, no matter how crazy it may be, can actually come true. You're going to have to work at it, and you're going to have to sacrifice. But your future, and the future of those you care about is worth it.

SELF-EXAMINATION QUESTION: There are a lot of challenges in building a network marketing business. Take a moment to visualize your Failure Scenario. Next, take a moment to visualize your Success Scenario. Are you going to let anybody or anything decide which of those two will actually become your future, or are you going to take control and decide that by the actions you take every single day?

CHAPTER 16

Setting Your Team on Fire

*As we look ahead into the next century, leaders
will be those who empower others.*

— Bill Gates

In the previous chapter, we discussed how to take your personal career to new heights. In this chapter, we'll discuss how to set any team, whether it's a company or a social club, completely on fire.

I love conducting corporate seminars and speaking at conferences, teaching these methods to entire companies. It truly does show the "power of the people." The Oxcart Technique is able to help dozens, hundreds, or thousands focus their passions on achieving what's truly important to them: their utmost desires that they are truly emotional about.

Aristotle said, "The whole is greater than the sum of its parts." This being true, imagine for a moment how strong the "whole" can be if the "parts" are operating at a much higher level. If the individuals are stronger, more focused, more passionate, more productive, what does that mean for the company?

If you can get each individual working at their highest potential, the impact on the team's overall performance can be staggering!

I find that all too often companies focus so much on the corporate vision statement that they neglect to, they fail to, focus on individual vision statements. What will really make the individuals on your team the most passionate about performing their jobs to the best of their abilities? What will drive them to work harder, better, and with more fervor?

Is it that the company will reach new heights? No, regardless of what the C-suite would like to think, that's most likely not that much of a motivating factor for them.

I was once with a $1.2B company that put together a huge 'Go Double' promotion, aimed at doubling the sales of the corporation. At their International Convention, they had huge 'Go Double' signage, and the corporate leaders led the entire auditorium of thousands of people in 'Go Double' chants. They even gave us leaders some silver Cartier bracelets with 'Go Double' engraved on them. Man, everyone was hyped up!

Did we 'Go Double'? Of course not.

People will not go above and beyond for a corporate mission statement, or for a goal to advance a company.

What's important to them is that they personally reach new heights.

Your job as a leader is to equate the two.

Focus your team members on how they can obtain the goals that are most important to them: their "carrot," and how they can avoid their "stick," by helping the organization reach its goals. Make them one and the same.

If you can harness this energy, this passion, this power — your team will be on fire!

It puts their jobs or professions in a whole new light. It's no longer about working for the paycheck, with a partial buy-in on the corporate vision statement — it's working for the things that are the most important in the world to them.

Imagine if all the members of your entire organization, from the ground up, were trained to harness the power of their most intense emotions. Can you envision how powerful that would be? Nearly any goal could be accomplished! Each individual would be propelled to new heights, to work harder and achieve more than perhaps they ever have before.

The energy flowing through them will flow through the entire organization, proving Aristotle right once again. The whole will, indeed, be greater than the sum of its parts. In fact, it will be far greater because each of the parts will be greater themselves!

In many cases, it won't be easy.

Early on in my business career, I joined a leads group. A leads group is a business networking organization such as Business Network International (BNI), where members attend for the sole reason of passing business leads back and forth and helping each other build their businesses. Four days after I joined the Chapter, the President of the Board of Directors asked me to his office, where he explained that there had been a big blowup on the Board, and the Chapter was going to fold—unless I took it over.

I was taken aback. I had never even been in a leads group before, much less led one. I was relatively new to the business world, especially compared to many of those who were on the Board of this organization.

But I knew people, and I knew what motivated them. Boy Scouts, the Corps of Cadets at Texas A&M University, and the United States Air Force had all taught me a tremendous amount about leadership and group dynamics.

My first step, I knew, would be to meet with each of the Board members privately, to see if I could get them to focus away from the infighting, and toward a common goal.

Without being obvious, I took each of them through an informal version of the Oxcart. I asked them what they wanted to get out of membership in the organization, what the benefits were to them — I searched for their carrot. Next, I asked them what the detriment would be to them if the organization folded — what their stick would be.

I then asked each of them what they thought we could do to patch the Board of Directors together to move forward — what an Action Plan would be. Because I solicited their input in coming up with the plan of action, I had their complete buy-in on the plan. It was their plan! Finally, after reviewing the points with them, I asked for their commitment. Were they committed enough to obtaining their Success Scenario and/or avoiding their Failure Scenario to follow their Action Plan? Each of them answered with a resolute "Yes."

As discussed earlier, merely talking about the goals and aspirations of the organization itself wasn't enough. They couldn't care less about the corporate mission statement or KPIs (Key Performance Indicators). They cared, as all of us do, about what was important to them personally. Again, it became my job to marry the two.

Then, and only then, could their emotions to reach their goals become stronger than the emotions that were holding them back.

The organization flourished. Each of the members, motivated by their own personal reasons, actively participated. A euphoria seemed to take hold as attitudes shifted and people became excited about reaching their goals, and helping others do the same.

Meetings were a blast, and new guests came weekly to see what all the excitement was about. We inquired as to how each of them would benefit from membership, focused them on that, and many of them joined our crazy group.

Within one year, we became the largest chapter in the entire state of Washington, and one of the largest in the entire nation.

About 18 months ago, I took over as the President of the Board of Directors of the Inland Northwest Council, Boy Scouts of America, a position dealing with a few thousand people, over a $2 million annual budget, and dealing with tens of millions of dollars in assets.

When I took over, we had recently dismissed our CEO and were without one, and at one point we were one-half of a million dollars in the hole on our budget, our numbers had been on a significant decline — which the exodus of the

LDS Church greatly accelerated — and we were in the middle of a crushing pandemic and a national sex abuse lawsuit.

To say that my new Executive Board and I had our work cut out for us is a grave understatement!

At the time of this writing, we're now well in the black, are upgrading all of the camps, creating significant new revenue streams, and, as a result, able to serve more kids than before — with that number climbing!

How? You've already guessed it: The Oxcart Technique. We got away from Mission Statements and Pillars of Success and all the traditional things that got us to where we were and started focusing on Success and Failure scenarios. As you can imagine, change was hard for a very tradition-based organization like the Boy Scouts. But as based in tradition as they are, they are even more passionate about turning young boys and girls into Honorable Men and Women.

In another recent example, the CEO of a medical billing company explained to me that his principal people just couldn't get along. There was constant bickering, in-fighting, and all the politics that can tear any organization down. He asked if I would help.

We got the team together and did two things:

1. Engaged in some team building exercises. The old adage of 'familiarity breeds contempt' no longer applies in modern team dynamics. The better you know someone, the more likely you are to trust where they're coming from.
2. Asked them questions that led them to building their Oxcart. When they came up with the Success and Failure Scenarios themselves, they internalized how important it was that they succeeded, and suddenly some of the pettiness fell away.

When people are focused on a goal they believe in, they're less likely to focus on others' faults. They're more interested in reaching the goal than tearing each other down. They realize that doing so takes them away from their goal.

What motivates the people on your team?

If we're talking about a business, we all too often assume our personnel are motivated solely by the financial compensation they receive, so that's all we concentrate on. After all, when they initially looked into the job, one of their first questions was, "How much does it pay?" So we offer them a raise every now and then, and perhaps some bonuses, and expect that they'll be inspired to give their best. Amazingly, we're surprised when they don't!

The pay may be the initial incentive that got them into the job, but the question is: What will keep them motivated for the long haul?

Remember the top nine answers to the question in the previous chapter: "What aspects of your job or business are the most important to you?"

As a reminder, they are:

- Being able to control aspects of my job or work environment
- Job security
- Relationships with my coworkers
- Money
- Opportunity to use my skills
- Opportunities for advancement
- The feeling I'm making a difference at my job or in the world
- Recognition/Appreciation
- Feeling that I and my opinion are valued

It becomes your job to find out which of these are leading motivational factors to each of your team members, and help them develop Success and Failure Scenarios and Action Plans that focus predominantly on those areas.

How do you find out what truly motivates them? Ask them!

That's right — simply take the time to find out what is important to them. All too rarely do supervisors invest the time to find out what is truly important to their team members. Those who do are often quite surprised by the information they receive, and by the simple actions that can be taken to provide a work environment that greatly enhances both morale and productivity.

The following very simple tool will help you do exactly that (click on "Job Employment Survey" button at the bottom of the screen to see the form on the next page — you may have to scroll down a little):

Name: Department:

JOB ENJOYMENT SURVEY

You are important to us, and so we want to produce the best work environment possible for you. To help us do so, please put the following in order of importance to you by placing the numbers 1-10 to the left of each of them. Only use each number once. Thank You!

_____ Being able to control aspects of my job or work environment. Why is this or is this not important to you?

_____ Relationships with my coworkers. Why is this important or not important to you?

_____ Opportunity to use my skills. Why is this important or not important to you?

_____ Money. Why is this important or not important to you?

_____ Opportunities for advancement. Why is this important or not important to you?

_____ The feeling I'm making a difference at my job or in the world. Why is this important or not important to you?

_____ Recognition/Appreciation. Why is this or is this not important to you?

_____ Job Security. Why is this important or not important to you?

_____ Feeling that I and my opinion are valued. Why is this important or not important to you?

_____ Other: _____
Why is this important or not important to you?

Now that you know what's most important to your employees, how do you use that information to their benefit, and to the benefit of your company?

As in the previous chapter, have each team member set up a Success and Failure Scenario based on what is most important in the world to them. Then help them establish an Action Plan as Barbara, our mortgage company owner in the previous chapter, did.

Your part in this is to ensure there are programs in place to support each of the areas that are important to the team members.

When "The Feeling I'm Making A Difference" is at the top of their list, establish a program that shows how they and your company are making a difference in the world in a way that is significant to them. When "Relationships With Coworkers" is high on the list, provide team-building opportunities to foster those relationships.

When "Recognition/Appreciation" is up there, put some money and focus into developing recognition programs. I can virtually guarantee you that any resources put into these programs will come back several-fold in employee satisfaction and productivity.

On this topic, understand this: No matter what number they put beside "Recognition/Appreciation," pretty much every single person on the face of the earth likes to be recognized. We love to be told we've done a good job. We want to be appreciated.

Many people will say they don't need recognition, and several of them will actually believe it to be true—but it's not. A simple "Thank you for a job well done," "You're important to us," "You're making a difference," and, most of all, credit for what they have accomplished, will actually go further for most people than a financial benefit.

The single best leader I've ever had the privilege of working with, Colonel Stephen Harper, would take the time out of his insanely busy schedule to handwrite thank you notes and congratulations every day. I still have some of them to this day. He even took the time to write to my mother and tell her what a great job I was doing! Can you imagine how motivating that was to me (and my mom)?

On the other hand, the single worst thing you could do is to take credit for someone else's work. Any leader who takes credit for others' work is no leader at all.

No matter the pay, work environment, or any other factor, morale will crumble if this happens. A wise leader, on the other hand, will quickly pass recognition on to those he leads.

On a trip to Hawaii a few years ago, I met a gentleman by the name of Victor Pigoga, the Director of Business Operations for EMC, an upper-level technology company. EMC had sent him on this trip as an incentive for a job well done. I congratulated him on his success and, without hesitation, he responded, "The congratulations truly goes to my team. I couldn't accomplish anything without them." With that single statement, Victor epitomized two of the top nine responses from our Job Enjoyment Survey above: Feeling Valued plus Recognition/Appreciation. Victor certainly values his team, and I would be willing to bet they know it.

Our final example in this chapter brings us back to our mortgage company owner, Barbara. After preparing her own Oxcart Action Plan, she sat down with one of her longstanding Account Representatives, Gary. Gary's job was to bring in new clients, and he had always done a good-enough job, but he wasn't exactly beating the bushes to find new business these days.

She discussed her newly energized vision with Gary, and asked him to join her in building a renewed excitement in the office. She described The Oxcart Technique as best she could, and even shared her Success and Failure Scenarios with him. She asked him if there might be a Success and Failure Scenario that he could come up with — something that might drive him, and she let him know she would like to help him achieve that goal.

She was surprised to see that his Success and Failure Scenarios had very little to do with money, but rather were focused on helping as many people as he could to get the best interest rate possible and get into a home where they could raise their families and build memories.

Gary was a bit taken aback by the effect that focusing his attention on that point had, as it brought back memories of him and his wife not being able to get into a house early in their marriage, and the disappointment and embarrassment that came with it. His reason for getting into the mortgage industry to begin with was to help ensure other young couples didn't have to go through that, if he could help them.

He now had a renewed focus and energy as well, as the long-lost passion began to rise once again to the surface, compelling him to reach out to as many people as he could.

Wanting to know how she could best help Gary reach his goals, Barbara asked him to fill out a Job Enjoyment Survey. Because it was so quick and simple, he agreed, and it gave her insight she never expected. As it turned out, she had been going about motivating Gary all wrong!

Here is that survey with Gary's answers:

GARY'S JOB ENJOYMENT SURVEY

You are important to us and we want to produce the best work environment possible for you. To help us do so, please put the following in order of importance to you by placing the numbers 1-10 to the left of each of them. Only use each number once. Thank You!

___1___ Being able to control aspects of my job or work environment. Why is this important or not important to you?

I like being treated like an adult & having a say in what I do.

___9___ Relationships with my coworkers. Why is this important or not important to you?

We get along fine.

___10___ Opportunity to use my skills. Why is this important or not important to you?

It's just not.

__5__ Money. Why is this important or not to you?

It's important, but the other things are more important than more money.

__8__ Opportunities for advancement. Why is this important or not important to you?

I'm happy where I am. I get to spend time with my family.

__3__ The feeling I'm making a difference at my job or in the world. Why is this important or not important to you?

I know that I'm helping my clients get a good deal, and get the home of their dreams – especially those without the best credit. Also, it would be good if we gave back to the community, somehow.

__6__ Recognition/Appreciation. Why is this important or not important to you?

It's not really. I know if I've done a good job. I don't need someone to tell me.

__7__ Job Security. Why is this important or not important to you?

It's important, but I feel my job is secure in the industry, either here or somewhere else.

__2__ Feeling that I and my opinion are valued. Why is this important or not important to you?

See number 1.

__4__ Other: Covered parking spot. Why is this important or not important to you?

It's hot in summer, cold in the winter-I don't like scraping my car windows.

Gary's Job Enjoyment Survey revealed what was truly holding him back: The fact that he felt he had very little control in the office was a demotivating factor for him, as was the fact that he had to leave his car windows cracked open in the summer, and had to scrape them in the winter!

It wasn't pay raises and bonuses that would motivate him to take increased action — it was having more control over his work environment, and feeling that his opinion would be listened to and acted upon. And, of great importance, that he was making a difference in peoples' lives. (A covered parking spot would be nice, too!)

These were elements Barbara could easily change, now that she knew the difference they would make for Gary.

Barbara's first priority: Knowing that Gary wanted to have control in his work environment and have his opinion valued, she realized she needed to sit down with Gary and solicit his advice on how to enhance productivity in the office. Although she could simply come up with ideas on her own, she knew Gary would feel valued being a part of the discussion from the beginning.

Judging by his responses, included in her discussion with him would be ways of giving back to the community and an incentive program for a coveted parking spot! She also solicited his input on a Recognition Program for the office. Even though Gary listed it lower on his personal priority list, she knew "other people" in the office would find it important, too.

Barbara performed the same actions with all of her employees, at every level of her company. As a result, the company began to grow again, and more employees needed to be hired. Before she turned much of the daily operations over to her new Personnel Department, she called in a team to train them on The Oxcart Technique and how to administer the Job Enjoyment Survey, as well, so they could interview all new employees and monitor the success of the programs.

By inspiring all of her employees to reach their goals, Barbara is well on the way to reaching her goal as well, and the world will, indeed, be a much better place.

EXERCISE: Fill out the Job Enjoyment Survey yourself, then give it to 5 different team members at different levels in your team. Are the results what you expected? Based on the responses, what actions can you take and programs can you implement to better fire up your teams?

CHAPTER 17

Retire Rich or Poor—Your Retirement Action Plan

If your ship doesn't come in, swim out to meet it!

— Jonathan Winters

This is a chapter that is near and dear to my heart. Very few things make me more sad than seeing impoverished elderly, barely scraping by after working hard all their lives, having to make the choice between the medications that will keep them alive or eating their next meal.

One of those people is my friend Helen. Helen worked hard all her life and had a meager savings built up. If she lived frugally, she assumed, she'd be able to pay her bills. She also assumed Social Security would help more than it did.

All too late, she wishes she would have saved up more, but there never seemed to be enough money left over at the end of the month to put much into savings. Now she's finding herself living in a way she never imagined. She doesn't really mind buying all of her clothes used at the thrift store, but it's going through the lines at the charity food distributions that brings her to tears.

Perhaps this is why I'm so passionate about helping people prepare in their earlier years, while they can still do something about it.

So many people are currently on the exact same path as Helen. It seems that so many things are draining money each month, and there's just not enough left over to pay all the bills, much less set up an investment account.

Many of them can even see it happening, but they aren't sure what they can do about it. Others are living with their heads in the sand, oblivious to their impending financial doom. Too many are convinced that nothing can be done at all.

That's why I'm so excited about this chapter: It lays out a plan to help nearly anyone develop a nest egg they can live with.

So how is it that people who work all their lives end up in poverty? There are many reasons, but a big one is "focus." We focus on only what's right in front of us, and the influx of media telling us we need to spend money on things that aren't actually important to us shifts our focus from smart, long-term investing to impulse spending for instant gratification.

The solution? We need to create a plan that focuses us where we need to be: preparing for our retirement.

That doesn't mean that we can't enjoy life right now, but it does mean that we need to be smart in how we do so.

How important is this? "Lack of a plan" is the Number 2 reason Yahoo Finance gives for "Why You're Not Rich Yet" in a July 31, 2013, article. (We'll talk about the Number 1 reason a bit later.)

It's time to develop that plan, and that's what this chapter is all about.

Another friend, Allen, is the best at this that I've ever seen — perhaps more of an extreme than is necessary, but it worked for him. Allen built an addition to his home and lived in it. He rented out his home, thereby paying his house payment and then some. He lived frugally and invested everything he could. At a comparatively young age, Allen is a multimillionaire.

Again, this may be an extreme example, but it illustrates what can be done. What your goals are, and what actions you are prepared to take, are completely up to you. The important thing is that you develop a plan, and that you act on it.

In one of my seminars, I asked people what their financial goals were for retirement. As you can imagine, the number of answers was about the same as the number of people who responded with.

I'll give you a number of the responses below, to help you think of what your goals might be:

- Travel with my husband, and spend time together doing things we want to do.
- Leave something to my kids. There was nothing left when my parents died, and I'd like to leave my kids something.
- Set up a fund for my grandchildren to go to college.
- Pay the bills.
- Leave money for a cause that's important to me.
- Be able to take care of my wife's medical issues. They can be pretty expensive.
- My wife and I have had a dream of going to Africa for as long as I can remember. We've always said we'll do it when the kids have grown up and gone.
- Donate money to women's rights groups.
- Buy land that I can turn into a wildlife refuge, live on, then donate when I die.
- Be able to afford good health care, so my husband and I get the best quality care and the highest quality of life we can have.
- I want to be able to continue to be active, in both mind and body. I want to be able to afford to experience new things, travel to new places.
- Wine. Really good wine. And good food. In Paris. And Boston. And anywhere else I want to eat or drink it.
- I don't want to ever have to clean my house again, or do laundry, or take care of the yard, or anything else that I don't consider fun. I want to be able to finally focus on me and do what I want.
- The 3 B's: a boat, some bait, and some beer.

All of these statements, no matter how big or how small, are each a goal. Most importantly, it's a goal that's important to the person who wrote it. That, frankly, is all that matters. If you attempt to write a Success Scenario based on someone else's definition of success, you'll never reach it. The entire time you are trying, your subconscious will be screaming, "But that's not what I want!"

To give you some ideas in writing your own personal Financial Success Scenario, let me give you an example from a wonderful man I met named Matt. Matt is in his early 30s and has three children with his wife, Sharon, whom he is madly in love with.

Because he is so young right now, he hasn't really been thinking about retirement yet, so he wasn't motivated to take the steps he needed to take, starting now, to have a happy ending to his financial story. When he developed his Success and Failure Scenarios, it gave him the kick in the butt he needed to set up a plan and stick to it for the long run. Here's his Success Scenario:

> I am 65 years old, and very blessed to be financially comfortable. I promised Sharon I'd always take care of her, and, after 42 years, I am still keeping that promise. We have dual medical insurance, so if the worst happens, our medical bills will be taken care of. Sharon and I have our same home in Chicago, so we can still play cards and go dancing with our friends, and a small home in south Texas so we can be near our children in the winter. Because of this, we have a great relationship with our kids, and we are also very close to our grandchildren. We've become an important part of their lives, so we can spoil them rotten and give them all the love we have in our hearts.

> We get to watch them grow up and to be part of it. We get to feel the warmth of them curling up on our laps as we read bedtime stories with them and giggle, and then they fall asleep in our arms as we hold them. We get to tuck them in, then tell our children how proud we are of them. We experience the joy of watching our children become the adults we always knew they could be. We have the opportunity to be there to still help guide them, yet still get out of their way and let them become their own people, making their own mistakes, learning from them, and having their own victories.

> We have just over 2 million dollars in investments, so, as long as we continue to live frugally, we can continue traveling overseas each year to help build homes, giving shelter to those who would otherwise have no hope.

We're saving children's lives each year through causes that are important to us, and we feel good that we're still able to make a difference in the world.

We enjoy camping in the national, state, and provincial parks across North America in our motorhome, and going to my reunions each year. We go to sleep each night knowing we don't have to worry about finances. As long as we keep our spending under control, we'll be just fine, and still get to do the things that are most important to us, as long as God gives us health and time on this earth.

THIS IS MY FUTURE. I WILL DO WHATEVER IT TAKES TO MAKE THIS HAPPEN. TODAY, I WILL TAKE THE ACTIONS IN MY PLAN SO I MAY ENJOY THE HAPPINESS I DESERVE.

What a great example of a Success Scenario!

Now it's your turn to write your own Success Scenario, based on what's important to you. As before, make sure it has plenty of detail and plenty of emotion!

You can start by writing down in list form the things that are most important to you. Next, write a story around those points, in the first person, and as if it's occurring right now. Be sure to actually picture yourself succeeding in the manner you describe.

Visualization is exceedingly powerful. You should find yourself smiling as you're writing this, maybe even crying tears of joy.

It's that emotion that will help continue to drive you toward success during the challenging times, when obstacles rear their ugly heads.

Can you get emotional about finances? Absolutely! It's not about the money itself —it's about what the money can provide for you and those you love. It's about security. It's about freedom. It's about being able to live your life and do the things that are important to you. But whatever you do, don't limit yourself. You can achieve far more than you may dream possible, even with limited funds.

On the other side of the coin is the Failure Scenario. This, too, needs to be detailed and emotional. Be honest with yourself. What would your worst fears be if you failed financially? Keep in mind that many of these worst fears actually become reality for a good percentage of the population of the world.

You can say that "failure is not an option," but if you don't take the appropriate action, it is a possibility. The reason you are doing this exercise is to make sure it's not a reality—for you. Again, "the stick" is a very important motivator, often more so than "the carrot."

When it came to the question about what most people feared for their financial future, again the answers were many and varied:

- To have to keep working until I'm too old to be able to travel or do the other things I want to do.
- My kids having to take care of me.
- To have to live in a facility where they don't take good care of me, and be left in my room or sit in a wheelchair all day.
- Be evicted from my home.
- Not be able to afford medication.
- Not leaving anything to my children.
- Not have enough money to take care of my husband's medical expenses.
- Not be able to go anywhere or do anything.
- A feeling of failing. Of failing at taking care of my love in her old age. Not being able to travel anywhere, or even eat what we want.

- Wearing old clothes because I can't afford new ones.
- To be embarrassed around my kids, because they know I'm poor.
- Not being able to leave anything to charity. There are a lot of causes that are important to me, and I'd like to be able to support them.
- Not be able to play golf.
- Have to move in with my kids because I can't afford my own home, or my bills.
- Not be able to pursue my passion anymore, because I can't afford it. My life would feel empty.
- To have to depend on someone else.
- Be one of those old people that people pity, because they're poor and have to live off of welfare. They have to put items back at the check stand and sometimes pay with change, because that's all they have. Their kids know they're poor, so they give them money sometimes, and it's so humiliating. They can tell that even their grandkids feel sorry for them, instead of respecting them and looking up to them. It's so sad.

When reading these, you can almost see a Failure Scenario writing itself, can't you?

I found the following story particularly sad, but very important to read to help inspire us to take care of our own financial future:

> I'm 66 years old and destitute. The worst happened with Tom's health, and we just weren't prepared. We hadn't invested enough, we didn't have the right insurance, and the funds have run out. I'm in a small, low income apartment, all by myself. I don't go anywhere or do anything, because I don't have my own transportation, and couldn't afford to do anything, anyway.
>
> My friends are all out doing things, and drop by sometimes, but who wants to come to this place anyway? I spend all day in this damned apartment; it seems like I'm doing nothing but staring at the walls, watching time pass. The kids are all hundreds of miles away. I can't go down to see them, and they're too busy with their lives to be able to come up here but maybe once a year.

I barely know what's going on with them, and I hardly know my grandkids at all. I can't afford to send them birthday or Christmas presents. I think their mom gave them something and said it was from me, because Jenny said, "Thank you for the Christmas present, Grandma" once. Either that or she assumed I had gotten her something. Either way, I got off the phone and just cried.

I don't know what to do. I'm so lonely here, and it's so cold. Last month, I had to sell the ring Tom bought me. It was my wedding ring, and the last thing I had of his.

Now it's gone, and I'll never see it again. It's probably melted down, along with all of its memories and meaning. But I had to buy my pills, or I can't breathe.

Even worse is that I'm almost out of that money, and my Social Security and Medicare just aren't enough to pay for what I need. I promised myself I'd never ask my children for help. But they'll shut off my heat if I don't pay my bill.

I just wish we would have saved more. But it's too late now. Nothing can be done.

As sad as that is, either one of the above is a very real scenario, all depending on the action taken. And, as much as you don't want to focus on the negative, there's more power in having something to get away from, in addition to having something to be moving toward. Just make sure you focus on the action you're going to take to avoid that possibility, and how good it's going to feel when you succeed.

As always, I recommend consulting experts to help formulate the points of your Action Plan. It may take a little extra effort, but you're doing this exercise to improve your life forever. In this case, you are making sure you have financial security when you need it, instead of being in the poorhouse. If taking the time to get a little advice improves your odds, isn't it worth it?

To help you along, we'll start by taking a look at the factors that make the most difference in people's finances. Each of them is completely obvious, but apparently not focused on enough — or there wouldn't be so many people having them as problems!

Simply put, in order to have more money for retirement, you either need to:

- Make more money
- Spend less money
- Or both!

An equation would be:

Money for retirement = (how much you make) minus (how much you spend)

Seems simple, doesn't it? Then why is it that so many people end up broke? In many cases, it's because they didn't have enough inspiration and motivation (the carrot and the stick) to put in enough perspiration (following their plan) to end in elation instead of desperation!

This is where The Oxcart Technique comes in, and why your personal Success and Failure Scenarios will give you the inspiration and motivation you need to stick to your Financial Action Plan.

Let's look at each of the elements in this equation in more detail:

MONEY TO RETIREMENT

Obviously, there are many factors that will determine the final amount of money you have by the time you reach retirement age, including return on investments, etc. That's where I prefer to bring in the experts as well, and that's outside the scope of this book.

The point we'll cover here is merely how much money you're putting into your retirement fund, not how you're investing that money. That being said, it doesn't matter what you do, if you have nothing to work with. If you don't put anything into your retirement account, you won't have anything for retirement! Conversely, if you have more to work with, there's more you can do.

So let's focus on creating the most money possible to deposit to your retirement, whether it's by making more money or by saving more money.

First of all, you might not believe you're making enough money right now to have a decent retirement fund.

In fact, according to U.S. News and World Report, the number one reason most people give for not saving for retirement is that they don't have enough money.

Hogwash!!!

My own mother was a widow who finished raising three boys on a nursing instructor's salary. When she passed away, she did so with over a million dollars in investments!

My own children at this point have very moderately paying jobs. But they're on their way to retiring as millionaires.

How are they doing it? Read on:

Remember the simple equation:

Money for retirement = (how much you make) minus (how much you spend)

To have more money toward retirement, you don't have to make more money. You can continue making the same amount of money, and just spend less. That will add to your retirement income. Will it add enough? Only you can answer that question.

So, do you want to make more money? The answer may actually be "No!" You may love what you do and not want to change. You've heard the old adage: "If you love what you do, you'll never work a day in your life." It's important for your well-being that you go to a job that you enjoy every day.

That job satisfaction has a direct bearing on your entire life! If you're not happy at work, you'll be less happy at home. It will have an effect on your relationships with your spouse, your children, everyone. And let's face it: These are most likely the best days of the best years of your entire life. You don't want to spend them hating your job and the people associated with it.

On the other hand, if you choose to, you can make more money than you're making right now. You simply have to figure out if it's possible to produce more income in your current profession, change professions to a more lucrative one, or (my favorite) create additional income streams.

The great news is, you can do one or more of these, make more money to add to your retirement, and enjoy having more money to spend right now, as well, if you like.

Because most people are comfortable where they are right now, I'm going to start by focusing simply on spending less money, freeing up more money to add to your retirement fund — which is exactly how my mom did it, as I mentioned earlier!

Option 1: Spend Less Money

The Number 1 reason Yahoo Finance gave for not "being rich yet" was that, "You spend money like you're already rich."

The truth is, it doesn't really matter how much money you make: If you're not controlling your spending, you'll be left with nothing! I can't tell you how many affluent individuals I know whose level of spending increases with their level of income. If you look in their investment accounts, you'll see that even they are going to bc in a world of hurt when they try to retire.

The truth is, we can choose to sacrifice now, or we will be forced to sacrifice later. Either way, we will sacrifice.

You may remember "The Ant and the Grasshopper" story from Aesop's Fables, where the ant works hard all summer while the grasshopper plays, and, come winter, the grasshopper has nothing to eat. I like to compare this to spending, as well. Those who spend all they make will be left with nothing, while those who sacrifice now will have something to spend in their older years!

If someone spends all their money on cool things right now, they might look cooler than you right now. But if you establish and keep to a retirement plan, you're certainly going to be the cool one later on, during retirement!

If your attitude is "Who cares! Live for the moment! Let tomorrow take care of itself!" you might as well stop reading this chapter right now. No matter how much you make, you'll keep spending it. But if you're ready to start building your future, read on —

Stopping the use of credit cards and paying them off is one of the most important places you can start, as money is getting sucked out of your account every single month in interest charges. It's like buying everything at twice the price! The problem is that when people attempt this, as with everything else, they start with good intentions, but their old buying habits come creeping back in, and they find themselves becoming less and less disciplined as time goes on.

In our society today, we're being told we "deserve" so many things, and credit cards enable us to get them before we've earned them. I'm here to say we deserve only what we can pay for! If we make the choice to have all of these indulgences instead of putting away for our retirement, then we can't expect someone else later on to pay for our bad judgment now.

Take responsibility for your actions, and take control of your destiny.

One of the best ideas is to set up an automatic deposit of a portion of your paycheck directly into your retirement account so you never miss it. Again, it seems to be universal that people will spend what they have.

A perfect example of this is John. John's in his mid forties, about 5' 10", and built like an army tank. When you shake John's calloused hand, you might as well be squeezing a boulder. He wears blue jeans, a T-shirt, and an unbuttoned long-sleeved flannel shirt on top of it—always. You know the type.

Here's what he told me:

> I'm a welder. I don't mean 'I do welding,' I mean 'I am a welder.' That's who I am. I've been welding since my daddy taught me at age 8, after his daddy taught him at that age, too. So it's in our family blood.
>
> I love making things with my hands, and I've never worn a tie in my life! I already told my wife: If you dress me up in a tie in my casket, I'll come back and weld the toilet seat up! I know I'll never get rich welding, but I don't care, 'cause that's what makes me happy.

You know what? I think John is right about part of this. This is exactly where he's supposed to be. Putting John in a different career field would be like putting a cat in water. It wouldn't be pretty — and someone is going to get hurt!

Maybe you can relate to him. But that doesn't mean he can't have a very comfortable retirement. He certainly can. He may not do it by earning more income, but, if we read on, we'll get some clues as to how he could build up a significant retirement fund.

He continues:

You can forget it. There's no way I could cut back on my spending to add to my retirement fund. We don't spend much as it is! But it seems the money goes out like water through a screen door.

I have my house payment like everyone, and I'm halfway done with my truck payment (though I'm probably going to get a new one soon). I have some pretty good tools, but they're all paid for. I can't afford to buy fancy gifts for my wife, Joy, but she's not that into jewelry and such, anyway.

We order pizza about once a week or so, and have to do the drive-through maybe about twice a week, maybe more, but it's not like we're going out for steaks every week!

Hey, the kids are in sports, Scouts, and everything else, and there isn't time to cook! Heck, even at the house most of our meals are those prepackaged ones, and we have to have snacks around.

We have three growing boys and a crazy schedule. With all of the running around, the gasoline bill is through the roof, but what are you going to do? You have to get kids where they need to go, not to mention running to the grocery store, the hardware store, and everywhere else. There's no choice in that!

Sure, the kids have cell phones, but we got them a cheaper plan. They're always going to practices, friends' houses, and all that, so we have to communicate with them. And we got them that unlimited plan, of course. That's how kids communicate these days.

My only vice is my TV channels. It seems like you gotta have all of them now to watch the shows and sports you want to watch! The way I unwind each night is some TV and a few beers—that's what does it for me.

That and my cigarettes, but don't even start on me about those! It's my body, it's my right, and I'm not doing anything to hurt anyone else, so don't go there. Not to mention, I'm down to only about a pack a day.

And, of course, my wife gets her Starbucks each morning. She can't operate without it!

So, look — the only expenses I have are the normal ones everyone has. I'm not spending like some rich guy, here!

But I sure don't have enough to set up any "investment portfolio." By the end of the month, there's not a whole lot left, and what there is, goes into our "date night" fund. That's important to me.

You know, while reading a story like this, it's easy to see where someone could cut way back on their spending. But John is actually very typical. He's not spending money on big-ticket items, but he's being "nickel and dimed to death." All of the small things are adding up to big expenses in the long run.

Ron Cavill, a Certified Financial Planner, has been a leader in the financial advisory field since 1969. His experience has ranged from the creation of three local investment advisory firms to upper management for one of the country's largest financial service companies. He has been a frequent guest on CNN Early Prime and has appeared on the CBS Evening News and on a number of PBS specials dealing with money and aging.

His #1 recommendation for his clients? Create a 3-month Cash Flow Statement.

According to Ron,

> The very foundation of all financial planning is understanding how much money you have coming in (income), and how much you have going out (expenditures). Most people really have no idea how they spend their money. They look at their income, and look at how much they have (or don't have) left over at the end of the month, and wonder, "Where does all of our money go?"

> Just as people don't realize how much they eat during a day, they don't realize how much they spend. It's not the big-ticket items, it's the small ones that happen throughout the day: a latte here, a movie there. Lunch out, dinner out; that thing they saw in an ad that "would make their life easier."

> When people map out exactly where they are spending their money, it's very revealing. They don't realize how much they spend that they really don't have to. The Cash Flow Statement shows them exactly where they can cut back, without it really hurting, to help them set up their financial future.

> I recommend doing it for a full 3 months because many times there are expenditures that don't happen every month.

The following are the categories I have my new clients provide data for. I ask them to provide both the Gross Monthly and Gross Annual dollar amounts associated with each category:

CASH FLOW STATEMENT

INCOME

- Individual 1
- Individual 2
- Miscellaneous
- Other

EXPENSES

- Alimony or Child Support
- Automobile (not including loan payments)
- Charity
- Child Care/Domestic/Parent Care
- Clothing
- Food
- Furniture and Furnishings
- Gifts (Birthdays, Weddings, etc.)
- Home Maintenance and Improvements

INSTALLMENTS OR LOAN REPAYMENTS

- Automobile Loans
- Credit Cards
- Other Loans or Credit

INSURANCE

- Automobile
- Disability Income
- Homeowners
- Medical
- Life
- Long-Term Care
- Job-Related Expenses
- Mortgage or Rent (not including taxes or insurance)
- Non-Reimbursed Medical and Dental Expenses
- Personal Allowances

- Real Estate Taxes
- Recreation and Entertainment (including dining out and online/TV channels)
- Schools (Nursery, College, or Private Tuition, etc.)
- Other Living Expenses (explain)

UTILITIES

- Condo or HOA Fee
- Electricity
- Gas or Oil
- Telephone/Cable/Internet
- Trash
- Water/Sewer
- Vacations

You can use Quicken, your credit card reports, or any other method you choose to find the information to complete your Cash Flow Statement.

The main point is: Give your finances the attention they require! We're talking about your financial future here —this is important!

It amazes me: If people are going on a vacation, they may plan it for weeks or months in advance. If they're buying a house, they'll research different parts of town and look through several houses before taking action.

But their entire financial future? Most people don't give it the attention it deserves and needs. They literally spend more time planning their vacation than their finances!

The result?

They're not where they'd like to be, and need to take action to get there.

Our friend John from the earlier example took this advice, and wrote out his 3-month Cash Flow Statement. He was astonished at what he found: Cutting back on one area alone could save him more than $150,000 over 20 years in just one category!

How?

John smokes about a pack of cigarettes a day. Now, before all you smokers out there get huffy (pun intended), I'm not here to argue the point of smoking or not smoking. Let's just talk about the financial end of cutting out one or two recurring expenses. (The exact same example can be given for high-priced coffee!)

John found that his smoking habit costs him about $6.20 a day in 2022. That's about $186 per month, or about $2,232 per year. That's a good percentage of his salary, and $2,232 per year he could be investing. Within 20 years, that $6.20 per day could be invested to make over $160,000! That's strictly talking about the cost of the cigarettes alone.

As long as he continues smoking, his health care costs will also be higher, eroding more of his potential savings. Keep in mind, that's just one part of his spending that could be shifted. There are many more areas John identified in his Cash Flow Statement that are enabling him to build a very nice retirement while still doing the welding job he loves so much.

I'm sure if you put in the effort to look at your personal Cash Flow Statement, you'll identify many areas where you can painlessly cut back, and add greatly to your nest egg.

What are some of the main areas where people waste money? Here are a few ideas to get you started:

- Gourmet coffee (regular coffee is much cheaper, and can be inexpensively flavored to tantalize any taste bud; the average gourmet coffee consumer could save over $1,000 a year or more in this area alone!)
- Gasoline (scheduling your trips can save you hundreds, even thousands, per year in gas)
- Name-brand groceries, name-brand clothing — name-brand anything!
- ATM fees
- New cars (even a slightly used car can save thousands)
- Credit card balances (move balances to a zero interest rate promotional card, pay them off as you can, and don't charge anything that you can't pay off the same month)

- Going out for drinks, fast food, or meals
- Unnecessary cellular plans
- Entertainment costs (TV/online channels, going to movies, etc.)

Do you see any items that you could cut down or cut out of your lifestyle? If you really take a look at where your money is going, and focus on ways to spend less, the amount of money you could save each month is astounding! Investing that savings alone can set you up with a nice retirement, virtually regardless of your income!

As pointed out by Sarah Carlson CFP®, CLU, CHFC, founder and financial advisor with Fulcrum Financial Group, and author of Facing Financial Fears: 8 Steps to Financial Freedom for Women:

Financial freedom is knowing what you own and owe, and living below your means. The bottom line is — spend only part of the money you have; don't spend any of the money you don't have. Respect yourself by paying yourself first, and do it every month by saving for your long term goals like retirement, as well as shorter term goals, like a new car. And always keep in mind: You will save more if you care less about what other people think.

The Chief Operating Officer of John's company is at a completely different economic level, but, as is true for many, his level of spending increased with his income. He made the same mistake most of us do: not understanding the difference between what we can afford, versus what we should afford.

As the number and price of the toys and privileges increased, so did his debt-to-income ratio, while his available funds for investing decreased. The result: lots of cool stuff, and a less-than-impressive investment portfolio.

He sat down with his financial advisor, who helped him identify places where he could cut back, if he chose, and his Scenarios gave him the continued motivation to do so.

Some of these were:

- Country club memberships
- Very expensive wines
- Leasing new luxury cars every year

- Eating and drinking out continuously
- 5-star vacations
- An extensive top-shelf wardrobe: Armani, Prada, Gucci, etc.
- Unnecessary lavish home upgrades
- Toys (jet ski, etc.) that rarely get used
- Unnecessary 'business' expenses
- Bad/risky investments
- Overly expensive hobbies
- Membership in private golf clubs
- Docking fees for large boat at a prestigious marina
- Membership in a private jet program

Because of his position in the business world, he felt he needed to project a certain level of success. Whereas a certain amount of that may be true, the bottom line is: You can only do what you can afford, and that includes having funds available to build a nest egg.

While still splurging in several areas, he has now curbed his spending to a manageable level, giving him the lifestyle he enjoys, while still preparing for the future.

John's neighbor, Saara, is a perfect example of how someone on a lower income level can take the right actions to develop a healthy retirement fund. Saara, a single mom of two, is a secretary. As a secretary, she only makes about $29,000 a year. But it's a stable job, and she gets off work not long after her kids get out of school, so it works out well for her.

Believe it or not, Saara is actually doing very well with her savings toward retirement! It takes extra work to make it happen, but she's choosing to sacrifice now, so she can enjoy retirement later. Her strategy is simple, but very effective:

"My Cash Flow Statement showed me exactly where I could cut back to have more money to invest. Here's what I'm doing: I buy as much as I can at the bulk food stores, and I've learned how to make meals from scratch. I save a bundle each month making my own soups and things, it's healthier and I enjoy it.

When I drive, I plan out how I'm going to take care of as many errands as I can each trip. My son is in Scouts and sports, but we carpool with some of the other parents when we can so we can all cut down on costs, and we actually have a great time doing it!

My television has only the basic channels, not only because of the cost, but because if my children are going to get scholarships, they're going to need to get great grades. Eating out isn't an option, but that doesn't mean we can't make fun meals at home as a family. And, if my son needs to call me, there's always another kid around with a cell phone.

I keep the thermostat down pretty low in my house in the wintertime, but not so bad that a sweater doesn't help. And I have to tell you: I'm a coupon-clipping maniac, and "sale" is my favorite word. I still go out with friends to parties and bars, or for coffee and such. But I keep a glass of water with lime in it in my hand all the time, so I don't waste money on expensive drinks. Besides, when my friends pick me up, we have our first drink at my house, where it's cheaper!

Savings? That's easy. It comes out of my paycheck every two weeks and goes straight to my investment advisor. I don't even see it. I just see the statement every 6 months that tells me how I'm doing toward my future.

Some of my friends think I'm a little extreme on some of these things, but you know what? They don't have much of anything saved up for retirement, and I do! So if "normal" is wasting money on all of these things and ending up poor, I don't want to be normal! I still have a great time — I'm just smart about it, that's all."

How does Saara keep up the enthusiasm to stick to her plan? You guessed it: She has her Failure Scenario, her Action Plan, and her Success Scenario taped on to her refrigerator so she can read them twice a day, every day.

We all have the power to decide on nearly any future we want for ourselves. We just need to apply all the tools at our disposal and take the action necessary.

So what did the Action Plan of our welder friend, John, look like? With the help of his new investment advisor, he set up a plan that was a bit of a sacrifice, but not so hard that he wouldn't stick to it in the long run:

John's Action Plan

- Set up $300 per paycheck to go directly into our investment fund.
- Transfer all credit card debt to zero interest cards, and continue to do that until they're all paid off.
- Stop using credit cards, and only have direct debit cards.
- Smoke only 4-6 cigarettes a day, working my way toward quitting.
- Drink only 2 beers a day, except on weekends.
- Help Joy make meals on the weekend that we can reheat during the week.
- Eat out once per week maximum.
- Schedule car trips so there is less running around on errands.
- Limiting to Prime +
- Have date night at home with Joy each week, and go out one night per month to congratulate ourselves for sticking to our plan!

Is that a plan that could work? Absolutely! It's simple, to the point, and not too painful. And most importantly, it gets John and Joy in the habit of focusing on what they're spending, cutting out some of the fluff, and putting it automatically into their investment account without even missing it. As time goes by and they find more ways to cut back, they can have more money come out of John's paycheck each time, while still enjoying life each and every day. Now, they simply do it more sensibly.

At the time of this writing, Dave Ramsey has a radio show on more than 600 stations with over 16 million listeners; and for good reason. His practical, common-sense approach has helped people around the globe make smart choices and take control of their finances.

His motto, "Debt is dumb, cash is king, and the paid-off home mortgage has taken the place of the BMW as the status symbol of choice," may not be the mantra used by everyone in financial circles, but I believe it makes an extremely valid point: We need to pay less attention to media and peer pressure, and more attention to prudent use of the money we make.

His website, http://www.DaveRamsey.com, is full of valuable information you can add to your own ideas to develop a strong Action Plan and to ensure that your Financial Success Scenario becomes your retirement reality.

Option 2: Make More Money

If making more money is of interest to you, you really have three choices:

- Find new employment that pays more;
- Make more money in your current job; or
- Create additional income streams.

Let's look at examples of each of these three choices.

Scenario 1: Find new employment that pays more

Amy is a hair stylist in her mid-thirties who needs to move on:

> "The truth is, I'm just tired of my job. I like the people all right, but this is getting me nowhere! I'm trying to raise two kids, and my husband is working all the time. To say money is tight is an understatement. We're barely paying the bills each month. In fact, some months we're not.
>
> When my youngest, Paula, jumped off the fence and broke her leg, that wasn't all she broke. She broke our bank account while she was at it. Cutting hair is all I know, though. My legs are so tired, they feel like they're going to fall off, but I'll probably be standing here for the next 20 years. I don't have a choice."

Does Amy have a choice? Of course she does! She is a perfect candidate for the "Do something else and make more money" plan.

In this case, Amy just plain needs to find a different career. She's unhappy where she is, because she's not making enough money. Sure, she could cut back on her spending, but the fact still remains: She's unhappy where she is!

Amy's Failure Scenario is easy: Ten years from now, she's still where she is right now, and still broke! And the next time something happens that requires more money, they'll go deeper and deeper into debt.

Her Success Scenario? She's in a new job, making more money. She's much happier in her new career, and advancing up the ladder! She's back to her old cheerful self, but something's still different: She's more confident and more in control than ever before. It's a stronger version of the old Amy.

How will she get there? That's where the Action Plan comes in. It may include night classes, getting a college degree or advanced certifications, or simply training for another career field. She can make a change and have a future she enjoys, because she's willing to take the action necessary.

It will take short-term sacrifice of extra work at night and whenever else she can fit it in, but it's a sacrifice she's willing to make. And her Success and Failure Scenarios will help keep her on the right track every single day.

Are you, or is someone you know, interested in finding new employment that pays more than your current job?

If so, EHow Money gives three great ideas to get you going:

> "First, visit the U.S. Department of Labor's CareerOneStop.org site, which offers tips about education and training, resumes and interviews, job search help, and salary information. Access to the information is absolutely free.
>
> Google your state's website for career counseling from the government. In the results section, search for the web address that ends in ".gov".
>
> Check your local community college for a career-counseling program."

Find a career path that you would enjoy every single day that enables you to earn, and invest, more money every month, and you'll find an Action Plan that will lead you to where you want to go: a beautiful Success Scenario that will change your life forever.

Scenario 2: Make more money in your current profession

If you enjoy what you're currently doing, you don't have to change jobs to make more money. You may be able to do it right where you are!

Carlos loves his job as a successful advertising executive, and he makes good money. Always dressed for success, he's the consummate professional. He usually goes to work early and always stays late. That "million-dollar smile" doesn't hurt, either.

"My challenge is that, even though I make great money, there doesn't seem to be enough. Mary and I don't spend excessively, we have no car payments, no credit card debt, but we have a mortgage, and, the most expensive of all: two kids in college. That's enough to break anyone! The money we had put away is going toward tuition and books now. Have you seen how much that costs? It's crazy! It's a lot more than we thought it would be. So, by the time that's over, there's not going to be much left for us. I don't know anything more that I can do. I already work 50 hours a week, and, in this down market, Mary's outside sales job isn't producing the income it used to."

The question for Carlos — Is there a way to make more money in your current profession? Odds are, there is. In Carlos's case, he went to his supervisor with the job description that he was first hired with. They discussed what he was currently doing above and beyond those duties, and rewrote his job description to better fit what he was doing now. He presented the updated job description to the Personnel Office who determined that it was, indeed, time for a raise. Naturally, all of these points were on his initial Action Plan.

He set new goals at work that earned him further income, and when he reached each of these goals, he changed his Action Plan to include new steps to reach the retirement that he and Mary dreamed of.

To develop her own Action Plan, Mary sought out sales people who were having more success than she was. Many of us know people in our professions who make more money than we do. The amazing thing is, if you ask those people what they're doing, they'll tell you! People love to give advice, and love to be listened to.

Mary used that guidance to develop her own Action Plan, coupled it with her Success and Failure Scenarios, read them out loud twice a day, and is now one of the top earners in her office. As you can imagine, her investment portfolio has grown considerably as well.

Scenario 3: Create additional income streams

Never before has creating additional income streams been such a possibility for so many people. Modern technologies and opportunities have helped level the playing field so practically anyone can truly live the American Dream — if they're willing to put in the effort.

With all my heart, I recommend reading Robert Kiyosaki's book, Rich Dad Poor Dad. It opened my eyes to the necessity and potential for someone with no business background to actually branch out.

There are countless opportunities out there, including real estate, network marketing, franchises, and so much more. Just make sure to research them well before getting started. There are also a vast number of scams and charlatans.

Whatever you do, don't limit yourself to your current skill set. Remember the Oxcart Parable at the start of this book? The farmer didn't have the skills to build a bridge, so he sought out an expert who taught him and helped him. You may, like me, need to develop a whole new set of skills completely outside of your current comfort zone.

My degree was in Mechanical Engineering, but I made my first real money in network marketing, or direct sales! How? I learned from people who were successful at it!

No matter how uncomfortable learning a new set of skills may be, is it as painful as your Failure Scenario? If the pain of your Failure Scenario is worse than the discomfort you'll have to go through learning a new skill set, then it's probably worth it.

Now it's your turn. You have an entire arsenal of knowledge at your fingertips that you didn't have before. You have examples, both good and bad, of others that may have been in the same circumstances as you.

So it's time to write out your Financial Success Scenario and your Financial Failure Scenario. Again, you should feel emotion as you're writing out the details of your worst financial fears and your highest financial dreams. As you're writing this, actually picture yourself in both scenarios. Write a story in the first person, as if it's happening right now.

Then decide which avenues you'll pursue in your Action Plan: Will you decide to spend less money, make more money, or a combination of the two? Either way, write out your complete, step-by-step game plan. If you're married, you might want to talk with your spouse about your plan.

Talk to those who are successful in a field you'd be interested in, even if it is the one you're currently in. Talk to those who are doing well financially in retirement age, and find out what they did to get there. I recommend finding a good Financial Advisor with whom you're comfortable, and get their advice, as well.

Then tape up on a wall (or something else that's vertical) your Action Plan and Success and Failure Scenarios, read them at least twice a day, analyze your progress sincerely, and begin setting up your own bright financial future.

You now have a game plan and the motivation to reach your destination. You are now in complete control.

SELF-EXAMINATION QUESTION: What are you going to have to sacrifice to reach your financial goals? What will you actually sacrifice long-term if you DON'T make those short-term sacrifices?

HEALTH

CHAPTER 18

Fit and Fine—Achieving and Maintaining Your Ideal Weight

The second day of a diet is always easier than the first. By the second day, you're off it.

— Jackie Gleason

"I arrived in Rome 'for a vacation of a lifetime,'" my friend and international weight-loss coach Gina Masoero explained. "I can't tell you how excited I was to be there, see the sights, and spend time with people I loved. In fact, I had dreamed about this trip for quite some time. And then disaster happened: My suitcase didn't arrive.

This would be a stressful situation for anyone — but for me this was a complete disaster! Most people can simply go to a department store and buy more clothes. When you're a woman who is almost 300 pounds, it isn't so easy. In fact, it's nearly impossible in Europe!

I absolutely can't describe the embarrassment I felt as I asked locals where any Plus or Queen Size boutiques were. Of course, they heard the word Queen and gave me that puzzled look we have all experienced when trying to understand someone with an accent. (Remember, things are often not called the same things in different countries.)

I then thought they would understand double or triple XL and when one person said triple X with their Italian accent, which sounded like 'Trip lay EEX lay — oh my gosh, you looka for clothes for a footaballa playa.' I thought that I would die! Here I was for four days, and I could not buy anything to wear. No coat—heck, I couldn't even buy underwear! Unable to find even a place to purchase underwear, I ended up washing and drying what I had every night in my hotel room.

Until that point in my life, I felt that I had it all under control! I had a successful business, my home was immaculate, my kids were raised and doing well, I was popular, liked, and respected in the community. What I wouldn't let myself realize is that I wasn't in control at all! Oh, sure, I looked like it from the outside. And in fact, I thought I was from the inside, too.

In my case, just like many people, it's not just that I had put my personal health on the back burner; I wasn't even in the kitchen! If I didn't put myself somewhere on my own priority list, I wouldn't be around to even have a priority list!

Things had to change!

I was excited when Terry asked me to give input to his book, because when I first saw him speak, I fell in love — no, not with him, but with The Oxcart Technique!

The first thing I said to him after his lecture was, 'Where were you and this Oxcart System 100 pounds ago?!' The morning after his seminar, I began calling family, friends, and clients I had coached, and I explained the technique to them. I had them write out their Oxcart Scenarios, because I found it so incredibly powerful to write out my own. In fact, I am going to share my actual Scenarios and Action Plan with you, to help you in developing your own:

MY FAILURE SCENARIO

I cannot believe that 60 is around the corner. I said that I would not be fat and 40. Then I swore I would not be fat through my fifties — and here I am, stuck!

I look in the mirror and everything has diminished with age, and I am afraid. Afraid that what I thought my destiny would be has come to fruition, that I am going to be fat my whole life. I am getting bigger every year and am a slave to prescription medications for high cholesterol, diabetes, and blood pressure issues.

The children are gone, married, healthy, happy, and have children of their own. I no longer need to bury myself in their lives. I love my career, but I can't attack taking care of myself with the tenacity I've attacked everything else.

What happened, when, and why? How did I get here? What is wrong with me? I have been fat and ridiculed since I was young — when is enough, enough? Where is the IT everyone talks about?

As a coping mechanism over the years, I have disconnected my mind from my body. I do not know how to pay attention and feel when it comes to myself.

PLEASE let me figure this out and break out of this prison called my body and mind! I am huge, unhealthy, stuck, and disgusted with myself — I have to change. I am going to die young at my own hand, and it makes me sick. I have so much to offer and am not living up to my full potential in this state of being.

MY FUTURE WILL BE DIFFERENT. I HAVE THE POWER TO ENSURE MY SUCCESS SCENARIO BECOMES MY NEW REALITY. I WILL DO THE FOLLOWING TO MAKE SURE I SUCCEED IN REACHING MY GOAL.

MY ACTION PLAN

- Upon waking up every morning, I will not jump up. I will lie still, getting conscious and in the present to keep me out of mindless auto pilot.
- Go through my mental checklist of the day and go "over my daily physical itinerary and commitments. Meetings; clients; appointments
- I will visualize what my day of positive choices will look like:

  - 30 grams of protein within an hour of rising.
  - My workout for that day.
  - Taking time between obligations and the day's commitments to eat.
  - I will get 7-8 hours of sleep a night and feel fantastic!

- Healthy fresh food is my medicine, and I will eat this way to stay off all prescription medications.
- I will give myself 110% with the same tenacity that I give and tackle everything else, because I am worth it!

MY SUCCESS SCENARIO

I am mentally and physically happy and healthy.

My daily positive choices reinforce everything that I stand for.

I am physically fit and choose a multitude of ways to get in my workouts.

My body moves with fluidity and things are not physically difficult.

I feel fabulous, take no prescription medications, and feed my body with fresh, healthy, non-processed foods!

I am physically able to do anything with my grandchildren, and it brings joy to my heart.

THIS IS MY FUTURE. I WILL DO WHATEVER IT TAKES TO MAKE THIS HAPPEN. TODAY, I WILL TAKE THE ACTIONS IN MY PLAN SO I MAY ENJOY THE HAPPINESS I DESERVE.

I can tell you that nothing in the world tastes as good as my Success Scenario feels. To know that I'm in control, that I'm in charge of my life, is the best feeling in the world.

Most of us don't think we're emotional eaters. We're wrong. When you're about to eat something, ask yourself: Why am I eating? Is it because I'm happy, sad, bored, angry? Disappointed? Feel like celebrating? There's only one reason you should eat: to build and maintain the mind and body you're dreaming of.

Now it's your time, your life, your future. You know you need to do this, and I know you can.

Get organized. Develop your own Success and Failure Scenarios, and create an Action Plan that you can stick to for the long run. Read them twice a day, every day, and take the actions to create the new you.

∾

I can't thank Gina enough for her kind words and wisdom. Most of us know what to do to achieve and maintain a healthy weight. Why is it, then, that people have such a hard time losing weight and keeping it off for the long run? The solution is simple for nearly all of the population: As in most things, it all comes down to motivation.

Knowing what to do and actually doing it are two different things. And then continuing to do the right things long term seems nearly impossible.

Keep in mind my saying:

> *The decision to succeed does not happen once.*
> *It happens every single day.*
> *In fact, it happens multiple times a day*
> *by the actions we take, or do not take.*

You are greatly influenced by what's motivating you at the time. If you're bored, watching TV, and that bag of chips is calling your name, then your hand going from the bag to your mouth is as automatic as breathing, and often at the same speed. You don't even realize it's happening. The siren song of that bowl of ice cream can pull you in like a ship to rocks. And alcohol? Don't even get me started! No, seriously!

Remembering that emotion is the driver of all action, we know that emotion often drives us to eat. Whether it's boredom, or stress, or celebration, or frustration, or a multitude of other factors that motivates us, we rarely overeat simply because we're hungry. And, keeping in mind that eating tasty foods (like a huge slice of moist chocolate cake with fudge frosting dripping off of it) feels good, it's also mainly an emotional response.

Looking at it from the standpoint of the carrot and the stick, we get pleasure from eating things we like. It feels good. It comforts us. It's often a reaction when we're nervous, depressed, or worried. Simply put: It feeds the pleasure centers of our brain. You can view this as our "carrot"—it's something we want to move to or to go toward.

Burning calories, on the other hand, is viewed by many as a "stick." It's something we want to avoid! We can use excuses like, "I just don't have time to exercise," but the truth is, there are other things we'd rather do or feel we have to do, so we do those, instead.

As in most things, we go toward the carrot and avoid the stick, and the result is an obesity rate that has grown to chronic proportions.

That's why reading your Success and Failure Scenarios twice or more per day is so critical. You have to keep that motivation first and foremost in your mind to have any hope of overcoming the temptation to tease your taste buds with tasty, tantalizing, tidbits of treats. Both the carrot and the stick have to work overtime to keep you true to your task.

In this case, you could even use a picture of yourself when you were at your ideal weight as part of your Success Scenario. The more you concentrate on it, the more that becomes your reality: "This is who I am."

There are many factors that make it harder for some to lose weight than others, such as low metabolism, genetics, child bearing, and other physical and mental factors. But this book is all about breaking through barriers; and history books, and the Internet, are filled with stories about people who have overcome obstacles—people who had the deck stacked against them and succeeded anyway. The choice is yours.

Let's start with your Success Scenario. Why do you want to lose weight, really? There may be many reasons, but you want to focus on the reasons that are the most important to you. Oftentimes, these can be very emotional reasons, and that's good.

It's the emotions, both positive and negative, that will help you make the right decisions and take the right action. Only if you feel these emotions strongly enough will you turn down that freshly made doughnut, still shimmering with warm sugar glaze. Only if you repeat your Success and Failure Scenarios twice a day will you get up early and exercise without skipping. It's motivation, both positive and negative, teamed up with information, that enables us to achieve our goals. It's the lack of motivation that allows us to fail.

When writing your Success Scenario, be sure to write a full account of what it will be like when you succeed at getting down to your goal weight. Tell what it will mean to you. Express the emotions you're feeling as you're around special people with your new body.

What will it mean to your activity level? How much more can you enjoy life? What will you do? You want to write as much "pleasure" as possible into your Success Scenario to help you when you're missing out on the pleasure that comes with your old eating habits. You need to see this as a much more enjoyable life.

And let me ask you this: Is it more enjoyable? Will it be worth it? Can you truly visualize how good it will feel to have less fat, be more fit, and be healthier overall? Can you picture yourself in your new body?

Visualize yourself at your goal weight, interacting with those you care about. Picture yourself with your significant other. Now picture yourself with your children or grandchildren, if you have them. Picture yourself doing something active with your friends. Please take a few moments to do this exercise before you read on.

∼

How do you feel right now? Doesn't that feel incredible?

Now, I know a good plate of fried chicken, mashed potatoes and gravy—lots of gravy—feels pretty darn good, but is it as good as the feeling you have right now? If you really took the time and visualized yourself, that food doesn't feel anywhere as good as the wonderful feeling that put that smile on your face. That's how your Success Scenario will help you do what it takes to reach your goals.

That's how it worked for Stella. Three children and too much overtime at her job kept her running way too fast to eat healthily. She called it "survival eating": shoving enough food in her mouth to give her enough energy to make it through another day.

She decided it was time to take control, and started by visualizing a Success Scenario that motivated her to make the changes she needed to reach her goal:

I am 55 years old, and look and feel powerful! I'm energetic and vivacious, a force to be reckoned with.

I continue to go to Zumba class twice a week. I lead the Girl Scout outings with all of the enthusiasm I had in my 20s, and help mentor those girls to become powerful, independent young women through the example that I set.

I golf 18 holes twice a week, because I can. Because my health is so good, I will be able to travel well into my 80s, and meet interesting people all along the way.

I'm able to enjoy everything that life has to offer, and meet it with all of the vigor of someone half my age.

THIS IS MY FUTURE. I WILL DO WHATEVER IT TAKES TO MAKE THIS HAPPEN. TODAY, I WILL TAKE THE ACTIONS IN MY PLAN SO I MAY ENJOY THE HAPPINESS I DESERVE.

This Success Scenario is extremely powerful for Stella, perhaps even more than a Failure Scenario would be. Stella has everything in there that she aspires to, and has the passion and belief to see it through. That's the power of a well-written Success Scenario.

As always, whether it will be the Success Scenario that is the main driving force, the Failure Scenario, or a combination of the two, will depend both on the person and on the situation—perhaps even on the day.

As in all cases, it's very important to write out an effective Failure Scenario, as well.

Again, this one may be, and should be, very emotional for you. What will happen if you don't lose the weight, and maybe even continue to gain more? What will happen with your relationships? What about the clothes you'll have to wear? What about your activity level? What will your health look like? What's the worst that can happen? Before you read on, take a moment to visualize that as well.

How does that feel? Probably pretty depressing. The question is, are you willing to take the action to make sure that never happens to you? Keep in mind, the decision to succeed isn't made once. It's made several times a day by the actions you take—or don't take.

William just turned 40, and, according to him, it was as if a light switch turned off. It seemed like his metabolism went into the tank, and his weight started creeping up like never before. The stress at work probably didn't help, either.

When his first grandchild turned two, he realized it had gotten to a point where he was having trouble keeping up with her—something he'd never experienced before. He tried every diet known to mankind, and they would work for a while, but he never seemed to quite reach his goal, and, over time, the weight would start magically appearing again on his body.

It was his Failure Scenario that gave him the kick in the butt he needed to knock down his three-beer-a-day habit, eat smaller meals, and add (gasp!) fruits and vegetables into his fast-food diet:

> I feel terrible. I've let my weight get out of control, and I can't stand looking in the mirror. I don't feel sexy, so I'm not sexy, no matter what Lori tries to tell me. Our sex life has just fallen by the wayside; it just isn't fun anymore.
>
> That's not the worst of it, though. My diabetes has gotten out of control! I have to take insulin shots every single day—I hate needles. I've seen people who have advanced diabetes when they have to have their feet and legs cut off because they don't have enough circulation.
>
> If this keeps going, I could be wedged in a wheelchair for the rest of my life, however long that is. I already don't have any energy. Forget playing with the grandkids—I can't even go for a walk without getting winded!
>
> And forget all the things I used to do, like hiking and skiing. Instead, I sit in my chair, gain even more weight, and eat more because I'm bored watching TV. My once-active life has come down to being trapped in my house, waiting for my life to deteriorate enough to get even worse.
>
> MY FUTURE WILL BE DIFFERENT. I HAVE THE POWER TO ENSURE MY SUCCESS SCENARIO BECOMES MY NEW REALITY. I WILL DO THE FOLLOWING TO MAKE SURE I SUCCEED IN REACHING MY GOAL.

It worked. These scenarios gave William the motivation he needed to reach his goal and make sure his Success Scenario, not his Failure Scenario, was his true reality—eventually. It wasn't easy, though.

After William reached his goal weight, he kept it off for a while, then decided he didn't need the motivation of reading his Success and Failure Scenarios any more. He was wrong. After a while, his weight started creeping back up again as his old habits came back to haunt him.

I realized, "What was I thinking? The Oxcart Technique is what helped me lose the weight to begin with, and helped me keep it off. Then I stopped reading my Scenarios and Action Plan out loud twice a day, and the weight started sneaking up again. What did I expect? I still need that kick in the butt to make sure I do the right things to stick with my goals, whatever they may be. Besides, it's free! It doesn't cost me a penny to do it!"

I believe that someday I won't need to read/recite my Scenarios every day — but that day isn't here yet! Until it is, I've started reading it all out loud twice a day again, and I've gotten back to my goal weight. And this time I've kept it off and feel fantastic doing it! It's amazing how empowering it is to be in complete control!

Nowadays, I don't let excuses or outside influences get in my way. There's no way in the world I'm going to let my Failure Scenario happen! And I'm darn sure going to live the life of my Success Scenario! It's my choice, and I choose to take the right actions to make sure it happens.

Before we go on to developing your Action Plan, have you noticed something? Here we are, in a chapter about achieving and maintaining your ideal weight, and I've riddled it with as many temptations as I could fit in about delicious descriptions of delectable delights. I've done everything I could to make your mouth water and get you to grab a snack.

Why is that? Because you're going to be tempted several times a day by things such as these. I want to condition you, starting right now, to identify these temptations for what they are: alluring sirens that will steal your goals and dreams.

A little too dramatic? Not really, when you think about it! I want to help you change your thought processes when these temptations come up and try to pull you down to your Failure Scenario, and give you the strength to break through them and achieve your goal of your ideal weight and all the great feelings that will be yours as a result.

As before, your first step is to write out your Success and Failure Scenarios, full of detail and emotion. Then it's time to set up your Action Plan.

There are many factors that affect weight loss, and the scope of this book isn't to develop your Action Plan for you, but to give you guidance to do so yourself. Each person's Action Plan has to be completely unique to himself or herself, or they won't follow it!

As in all things, I very much recommend consulting the experts. I don't advocate starting any kind of weight management plan without consulting your doctor. A nutritionist and personal trainer are also great resources in helping you develop your Action Plan.

Depending on your circumstances, you might find a psychiatrist or hypnotist helpful. Never underestimate the mental aspect of any goal. There's great free advice online, but make sure it's from reputable sources. Let the experts give you the advice you need to establish a daily Action Plan you can live with, and possibly live a lot longer with.

Then, please keep in mind that everything should be done in moderation. For instance, you don't have to cut out sweets completely — just cut down on them. Don't start out running marathons on your first day. Maybe start by walking down the street. If you develop an Action Plan you won't stick to for the long run, you're setting yourself up for a yo-yo diet. If you set up an Action Plan that can be your new lifestyle, the ongoing motivation from your Success and Failure Scenarios will help it become exactly that.

The following are ideas that you can draw from when developing your own personal Ideal Weight Action Plan. Keep in mind that you don't have to do all of these ideas. In fact, if there are some that you know you probably won't do, it's probably best not to include them in your plan. If you neglect one part of your plan, it may feel like failure and cause your subconscious to say, 'I'm not doing this point, why should I do the others?' It's important to set up a Plan that you can, and will, stick to:

- Eat healthier.
- Consume fewer calories.
- Do aerobic workouts. Start slow. Make it fun.

- Use stress-relieving techniques such as yoga, meditation, or other ways to alleviate stress in your life, or at least give you a break from it.
- Eat smaller meals more often.
- Prepare meals on the weekends for the week ahead.
- Eat fewer sweets and other simple carbohydrates.
- Stop drinking sodas.
- Reduce alcohol intake.
- Eat slower.
- Drink plenty of water, especially before meals.
- Eat only when you are hungry.
- Eat a healthy snack whenever you're hungry, but not just because you are bored or stressed.
- Take healthy snacks with you wherever you go.
- Add more exercise into your daily routine whenever possible. Walk more, sit less.
- Read restaurant menus online before going, so you can make healthy, non-emotional choices when you get there.
- Share meals at restaurants.
- Eat breakfast to get your metabolism going.
- Take healthy nutritional supplements.
- Monthly, reward yourself with a non-food incentive for sticking to your plan!

It's important to make long-term lifestyle changes that you can and will stick to. It's a marathon, not a sprint. Most people gain the weight back after they've reached their diet goals because they had a short-term approach to weight management. They set up a weight loss plan, but no long-term weight maintenance plan.

It's critical that you do both, and continue to monitor your progress for the long term.

What actions will you continue to take once you've reached your goal weight or size? What actions will you modify so you maintain a healthy weight?

Your Action Plan must include these things to ensure long-term success, and you'll need to read/recite it at least once a day for the long term, to make sure you don't fall into old patterns.

Will this take effort? You bet it will! Will it be worth it? If you're in doubt, go back and read your Success and Failure Scenarios. That should answer the question for you.

Can you do it? You have complete power over your actions, and, properly motivated, I believe you can accomplish virtually anything!

Ok, enough reading.

Get to it.

It's time to make a positive change in your life!

SELF-EXAMINIATION QUESTION: How do you truly feel about your current health? What will happen if you don't change it? Thinking of all the people in your life, and things you'd still like to do, how will all of that be affected if you don't take action and do something about it?

CHAPTER 19

Overcoming Any Addiction

*Always bear in mind that your own resolution to
succeed is more important than any other.*

— Abraham Lincoln

I almost cut this chapter completely, as it seems so far from the scope of this book.

Then one day my doorbell rang, and the need to keep it in this book became exceedingly apparent.

I opened my door to see a member of the team that cleans my house.

"Oh, Mr. Fossum," she said, "I'm so sorry to bother you, but I think I left my sweatshirt over here when we cleaned two days ago. I was wondering if you've seen it."

"I haven't seen anything," I replied, "but I don't go everywhere in the house. You know the place better than I do, so come on in and look around!"

Something felt odd, though. I had no reason to suspect her of anything; she had been to my house several times before, and was often by herself in the various rooms. And she was always fun to chat with, with a bubbly personality that makes her immediately likable.

But her demeanor just seemed different this time, a little anxious. Plus, add to that the fact that she didn't call first, she just showed up at the door, and that she was wearing a baggy sweatshirt that she could easily hide something in — it just felt a little odd.

I crept up the stairs to where I could see through our bedroom suite to our master bath, and I was shocked to find her looking in one of my drawers!

"Your sweatshirt won't be in my drawer," I said as I announced my presence.

"Oh! No, the drawer was open so I thought I'd shut it for you! Oh, look — there it is, over there!"

She motioned over to my bed, where her sweatshirt lay half under my bed—a bed that I had made the day prior. There had been no sweatshirt there at that time.

I decided not to confront her at that moment, but to talk with my wife first, to confirm that there was no sweatshirt by her side of the bed.

Her response: "If there was another woman's clothing by our bed, I would have noticed it!"

Fair enough.

Next, I called up the owner of the company and told her what had transpired. "I believe she was robbing me. As a result, she won't be in my house anymore, and I'm changing all of the security codes. If she was robbing me, she is most likely robbing others, and you need to consider whether or not you're going to keep employing her."

The following day, the owner called up with the employee on the line, in tears and apologizing. She had immediately come clean. "I'm so sorry. I'm so sorry. I was looking through your drawers for your prescription pain pills. 12 years ago I was in a car accident. I have fibromyalgia and chronic pain syndrome, and I've been addicted to painkillers ever since. I've been hiding my addiction from my husband and everyone else for over 13 years. You're the first person to catch me. I'm so sorry!"

I knew I needed to help her. Not enable her, but help her. It was time to apply the Oxcart Technique.

First step: The stick, or Failure Scenario, so I laid it on her: "Okay, you were stealing my prescription pain meds. That's a felony. You're going to prison."

And I let that sink in just for a minute, then continued with her Action Plan: "Unless. Unless you check into inpatient drug rehab immediately, followed by an outpatient program. And I'm going to send you a draft of the book I'm writing on the Oxcart Technique. I want you to do what it says."

"Absolutely, absolutely! I will right away! I promise"

"That's good to hear, but know that I will be following up with you. I will be keeping track of your actions, so I know you are actually getting the counseling you need. And I want to keep in touch with you."

Now it was time for the carrot, or her Success Scenario: "And then, if you do these things, you can finally be free! You can stop lying to your husband. You can stop lying to your friends and family. You can stop lying to yourself. And you can be proud of yourself and the life you're living once again."

"That sounds great! I will do it, I promise! Thank you so much for understand! Thank you so much!"

~

If you are suffering from an addiction, I want to sincerely congratulate you for taking the first, perhaps most critical, step: recognizing it and wanting to do something about it. It takes more courage than many people have, by themselves, to take the steps necessary to regain control.

And that's really what it's all about, isn't it? Control?

Wikipedia defines addiction as "continued repetition of a behavior despite adverse consequences."

Whether it's tobacco, abusing alcohol, drugs, gambling, sex, pornography, video games, or whatever it is, right now the addiction is controlling you. It's controlling your actions. It's controlling your destiny.

You are going to change all that.

It's critical to say right up front that willpower alone may not be enough. Most people require professional help.

That being said, without willpower, there's no way in the world you're going to overcome your addiction.

Facing an addiction can be one of the most daunting tasks you'll ever face. Since your brain chemistry has been altered to build the addiction, it will be necessary to re-alter it to bring it back to where it was before the addiction began. The bad news: Depending on the individual, it may be very hard to break the addiction. This may take determination, work, and persistence. The good news: It can be done, and you CAN do it.

In fact, most people do.

It seems to be public perception that it's abnormal to kick an addiction. Nothing could be further from the truth! According to an article written for CNN by Dr. Marvin D. Seppala, literally "most people who have used cocaine or heroin have quit ... 60 percent of smokers have quit."

What does this mean? It means the odds are very much in your favor! You're not fighting a losing battle — you're fighting a winning battle! Most people who are in your position have kicked their habit and overcome their addiction.

But what exactly is addiction, and why does it affect us as it does? Dr. Seppala's article goes on to say:

We know that addiction resides in the limbic system, a subconscious part of our brain that is involved with memory, emotion, and reward.

We refer to this area of the brain as the reward center, as it ensures that all rewarding or reinforcing activities, especially those associated with our survival, are prioritized. The reward center makes sure we survive by eating, drinking fluids, having sex (for survival of the species), and maintaining human interactions.

In late stages of addiction, we can see how reward-related drives, especially those for survival, are reprioritized when people risk their families, their jobs, even their lives to continue to use drugs and alcohol. The continued use of the drug becomes the most important drive — at a subconscious level and unrecognized by the individual — undermining even life itself.

So what does this all mean? It means that whatever someone is addicted to can become more important than everything else. They'll play video games instead of getting work done. They'll view pornography at the expense of their marriage. They'll smoke cigarettes or abuse alcohol no matter the effects on themselves or those around them. The need for the next drug fix may outweigh even their own children's lives.

This is where it becomes critical to reprogram your brain to put those priorities back where they should be, and where the Success Scenarios and Failure Scenarios are absolutely critical for doing that.

For many addicts, the necessity of being given the hope of what their Success Scenario can look like twice a day, every day, may be enough to help them push through the challenges. Many may need their Failure Scenario kicking them in the side of the head to help force them to take the appropriate actions and to stay away from the inappropriate ones.

What are those appropriate and inappropriate actions? Obviously, the appropriate actions are those that will take you toward your Success Scenario of breaking the addiction. What are the inappropriate ones? You guessed it — those that take you toward your Failure Scenario.

What those actions are specifically may be too varied — depending on the individual, the addiction, and the circumstances — to even begin to cover them in this book. This is where professional help must be sought in the form of an addiction specialist, clinical social worker, or others to help you develop a plan that will work for you.

You must undertake your quest with the understanding that the common path to recovery is not a straight path, but a path that contains twists and turns in the form of challenges, relapses, and setbacks.

You may not make it on your first try. And please understand: THAT'S OKAY!

In this case, as in all cases, it's critical not to view the Failure Scenario as having been permanently reached every time there is a relapse, but rather to view those relapses as stepping stones to eventual success. Let's face it: We all mess up on occasion. The difference lies in whether we see that as permanent failure or understand that we have to, once again, dust ourselves off, get back on the path, and continue to strive to push forward.

There's a Chinese proverb that says, "Failure is not falling down, but refusing to get up."

You could even consider having a point in your Action Plan that says, "If I do have a setback, I will not view it as permanent. It is merely a temporary road bump on my path to recovery. I will forgive myself and take the steps necessary to help avoid it in the future. I will step out again with courage on my road to Success."

So let's take a look at a couple of Success and Failure Scenarios:

Scott has been smoking for over 40 years. He started in the military ("Smoke 'em if you've got 'em!") and has been smoking anywhere between a half a pack and two packs a day ever since. Given that Scott is a rough-and-tough man's man, there's not a person out there who could convince him to quit, and they'd better not try! Lately, though, he's been becoming short of breath. Hiking with his grandchildren is becoming impossible. He's getting pretty ticked off at not having the energy he used to have, and he's finally come to the conclusion, on his own, that it's time.

He was kind enough to share his Failure Scenario with us:

> I'm 70 years old, and I have to carry an oxygen canister with me wherever I go. I'm too short of breath to walk down the hallway, much less down the street.
>
> My legs work fine, but I have to use one of those (darn) carts just to get around. My grandkids see me as an old, frail man instead of the man I used to be, and still am in my mind.
>
> Instead of doing things myself like I've always done, I have to get help just to do the simplest chores. No more dancing. No more golfing. No more chopping wood.
>
> MY FUTURE WILL BE DIFFERENT. I HAVE THE POWER TO ENSURE MY SUCCESS SCENARIO BECOMES MY NEW REALITY. I WILL DO THE FOLLOWING TO MAKE SURE I SUCCEED IN REACHING MY GOAL.

Not a great potential future, and it certainly creates strong enough emotions in Scott to help him stick to his Action Plan set up for him through his smoking cessation program. His Success Scenario is also helping keep him on track:

I'm 70 years old, no longer smoking, and am getting some of the energy back that I had years ago. My grandkids don't tell me I smell like an ashtray anymore. If they did, I could chase them down and tickle them until they took it back!

My golf game is strong, and I'm still attracting the ladies on the dance floor. I'm able to take the dogs on walks through the woods, and enjoy all that life has to offer.

THIS IS MY FUTURE. I WILL DO WHATEVER IT TAKES TO MAKE THIS HAPPEN. TODAY, I WILL TAKE THE ACTIONS IN MY PLAN SO I MAY ENJOY THE HAPPINESS I DESERVE.

To add emphasis to his scenarios, Scott taped pictures of his grandchildren and his favorite golf course, along with pictures of his favorite dance partners. Not only do they help keep him on track, they make him smile every single day.

A new addiction is beginning to surface in society as a major problem: an addiction to video games.

Remember Wikipedia's definition of addiction as "continued repetition of a behavior, despite adverse consequences." People are ignoring their occupational obligations or their schoolwork because of video games. They're putting healthy relationships lower on the priority list than gaining status in their game. They're ignoring chores, responsibilities, even their own families! The make-believe world in the game starts taking precedence over their real world.

How can this be? Why would a child, or an adult, continue to play even when the truly important aspects of their lives are falling apart?

It's quite simple: Video games are designed to be highly addictive.

Video games give immediate gratification. They hit the pleasure centers of the brain. According to Laurel Quast, a 30-plus year clinical social worker from Santa Rosa, California: "Video games provide escapism from the problems or challenges that a person may be facing in their actual life. They provide a sense of empowerment that may be lacking anywhere else. It's a condition called 'Process Addiction.'"

In the journal *The Professional Counselor* (2014), authors Wilson and Johnson cited Sussman, Lisha, and Griffiths's 2011 definition of Process Addiction: "It is defined as any compulsive-like behavior that interferes with normal living and which causes significant negative consequences in their family, work, and social life. Gambling, Internet addiction, sex addiction, exercise addiction and eating addictions are among those identified as PA" (p. 1).

What can be done about it? As usual, there are many options, and a professional should be consulted to help overcome any addiction.

But a major weapon in your arsenal in establishing the want, the need, to overcome an addiction is the creation of your Success and Failure Scenarios. These will give you the motivation to establish a plan, and stick to it in the long run.

Your brain sees all of the factors that feed your addiction as a carrot, or something pleasurable to go toward. Therefore, you'll need to develop a stronger carrot in your Success Scenario, coupled with the powerful stick described in your Failure Scenario, to help override the impulses that might otherwise overpower you and take you off your goal of overcoming your addiction.

Let's use 18-year-old Victor as an example. According to his mom, he's used to getting pretty good grades without really trying, and gets in a little trouble at school, but nothing really serious. The problem has come up in the last year or two, with the introduction of a brand-new video game that has to remain nameless here.

Let me tell you this, though: It's an awesome game! Lots of action, seriously cool graphics, and, best of all, he can actually play it online with his friends, or with other people around the world! At school and everywhere else, all the kids are talking about it. They compare notes, or talk about games they played together.

Here's the problem, though: All Victor wants to do is play this game. He continues to nag his parents to let him play more. Just as he's finishing high school, his grades are starting to fall, chores are not getting done, and a social life outside of that game is becoming non-existent. This is the fine line where a hobby becomes an addiction.

Victor's Success and Failure Scenarios were pretty easy to see: Without good grades, his chances of getting into a good college were dropping. Without good work habits, his chances of getting and holding a good job were rapidly decreasing, as well. He needed both of these things to get a good start on the rest of his life.

The solution? Moderation. Victor and his parents worked out an Action Plan that included doing homework every night to get those grades up to where they needed to be, and getting chores done first. Then, and only then, he could play his game for a limited amount of time.

You know what was interesting? As he played it less, he wanted to play it less. It didn't seem that important. He found friends who talked about something other than the game. He actually got involved in a couple of other hobbies with more activity and interaction that he enjoyed. He broke the addiction.

Does he still play sometimes? Sure! But does the desire to play it control his life? Not anymore.

Some people walk away from an addiction easily. Others need more help. All of them need a game plan, and the motivation to make it happen.

Perhaps no one knows this better than Katherine O'Connell, who has been a Registered Nurse since 1995, and has worked in an addiction detoxification unit since 2008. She has seen the results of long-term drug addiction on her patients, ranging anywhere from neglect of life and loved ones, to liver failure, to complete encephalopathy, where the patient's brain becomes nearly useless, capable of only the most basic functions.

Katherine has seen some patients gain control of their addiction, and some patients that, by their own choice, never will.

She was kind enough to share her insights of some critical steps that can mean the difference between success and failure for someone with a chemical dependency:

> You have to recognize and admit you have a problem. Stop lying to yourself and others. It doesn't help. It's time to start telling the truth, so you can get better.

Decide you truly want to change, and are willing to take the actions to change. Write out your Success and Failure Scenarios, and take a good look at how bad your life can be if you don't change, and how good your life can be if you do. Don't let the Failure Scenario depress you, but rather use it as a kick-in-the-butt to make a change.

Get professional help, as well as ongoing counseling. I know it's expensive, and alcohol/drugs are cheaper in the short run. But counseling is the most important place you could possibly spend your money. You need to do this. Among their normal procedures, ask them to help you develop your Oxcart Technique, making them part of the process. They can help you create your Action Plan to help make sure your Success Scenario is your new reality.

Stay completely away from any friends or acquaintances that use drugs of any kind. The temptation to use can be overwhelming. Too many addicts think, "Just once won't hurt." The process can start all over again. You must stay away from enablers. I've actually had family members bring alcohol to patients in our detox unit. If there are enablers in your life, it is up to you to stay away from them. You must be strong.

Get to the root of the problem that may be behind the addiction to begin with. Are there personal issues that are causing stress? Are there psychological issues that have not been dealt with? Figure out what the problem is, and deal with it directly. Again, your counselors can help you do this.

"Be extremely careful not to replace one dependency with another; it's a common occurrence. Some smokers become overeaters. Drug addicts become alcoholics. This is why you must get to the actual root of the problem that is causing your addictions, not just dealing with the symptoms."

Tape your Success and Failure Scenarios and your Action Plan where you can see it every day. Twice a day, read it out loud, just like this book describes. This may greatly help you keep focused and on track.

Have a sponsor and a backup sponsor available 24 hours a day, 7 days a week. Make the conscious decision, and one of your points in your Action Plan, that you WILL contact your sponsor the second you consider using drugs, and make sure your sponsor has a copy of your Oxcart Technique to help you stay focused on your long-term goal of staying clean and having a better life.

It may not be easy. It may be very hard. But it affects the rest of your life, and the lives of the people around you. It's worth whatever you have to do to make it happen. Make the decision — and just DO IT.

That decision wasn't easy for my housekeeper that I mentioned at the start of this chapter. But the moment I caught her stealing my prescription pain pills was a critical turning point in her life.

She was finally forced to face her addiction and to do something about it or suffer some pretty terrible consequences. With the threat of being reported to the police, she had a really big "stick," or Failure Scenario, staring her right in the face. And that's what it took.

She checked into and completed a several day inpatient detoxification. After that, she joined a group therapy session and worked with her psychiatrist as well as her drug addiction counselor and a new medical doctor. Being deeply in debt, she was extremely concerned about the $6,000 this would all cost, but her supportive husband simply assured her, "Don't worry about it. We'll figure it out."

We worked on her Failure Scenario together, which included losing her husband, her children, her freedom, everything. It also included overdosing, and potentially dying.

"There's absolutely no way in the world that I'm going to let any of that happen," she adamantly assured me. "I WILL do what I need to do to stay off of the painkillers forever, no matter what."

Her Success Scenario was a bright future that had seemed impossible just a few short weeks before. It includes paying off all the debt she accrued from buying all the pain medications, and even having money in her wallet. She dreams of spending time with her husband, and even being able to travel with him. She dreams of a drug-free future.

She understands that it won't be easy, but that her Success and Failure Scenarios will help her stay on track every single day.

How will it go? There's no way to tell. "I take it one day at a time, and I don't try to overdo things," she says.

I can tell you that she has recently secured full-time employment as an office staff member, and she hasn't taken a pain pill since the day after she left my house.

In fact, the night before I was going to send off the final draft of this book, I received this email from her:

> I wanted to give you a brief update as to what I've been up to. I just started my new job yesterday. I absolutely love it. I am being trained to run the entire office. For now, I am going to be working two jobs. It's exhausting, but for now I know I can do it. Recovery is going so great. I feel like my old self, but so much better. I have energy, focus, and drive.
>
> I really hope everything is going great with your book. People are going to love it and benefit so much from it.
>
> "My Best to You and Your Family. =)"

She told me just a few days ago, "I know it sounds funny, but I thank God you caught me that day. It was a day that changed my life for the better — forever!"

If you, or someone you know, is struggling with an addiction, I pray that this chapter is helpful in creating a bright, addiction-free future where you can enjoy all that life has to offer.

It can be done, and you can do it!

SELF-EXAMINATION QUESTION: You shouldn't fight this battle on your own. Who are you going to seek help from? I know this may be painful or embarrassing. Is avoiding your Failure Scenario and achieving your Success Scenario worth it – if not for you, but for the people around you?

RELATIONSHIPS

CHAPTER 20

"If Mama Ain't Happy..."
Breaking Through to a Happy Marriage

*Many people spend more time in planning the wedding
than they do in planning the marriage.*

— Zig Ziglar

There's a reason I saved this chapter for last. I absolutely believe that your marriage is the single most important goal in your entire life.

No matter how much money you make, or how many things are going great in your life, if you're having emotional challenges with those who are close to you, it can be all-consuming. It's been said: "If mama ain't happy, ain't nobody happy." And that goes for papa, as well.

For those of us who are married or in a serious, committed relationship, that relationship is the pivotal one. There may be many people who are close to us, but this is the person whom we are closest to in the world. If that is not the case, it's a relationship that needs some work. If it is the case, it's a relationship that's worth working on to keep it going well.

As you probably know, marriages take an enormous amount of work, and they're perfect only in storybooks. Let's be completely honest here:

"Happily ever after" doesn't mean "Happy all the time."

There will be disagreements and disappointments, disputes and despair. Odds are, there will be conflicts over money, sex, how to raise the children, where to go on vacation, untidiness, chores, decision-making, and pretty much everything else you can think of!

If you're new to a marriage, or even if you're not, understand this: This is the way it is. Pretty much every happily married couple you know has gone through and continues to go through emotional challenges. You're not alone. It's not just you two. All of us have gone through it, and you're not immune, no matter how much in love you are.

It's not about that. It's about the fact that, happily, you are two different people with your own views of the world. Those views will clash from time to time. I would certainly hope so! Otherwise, one of the two of you isn't being honest about your beliefs.

Does it mean that you don't love the other person if you disagree with them? Of course not! And it doesn't mean they don't love you — even if they're acting like such a stubborn jerk right now that it makes you wonder!

The road to happiness has many twists, turns, and bumps along the way. How those conflicts are handled makes all the difference in the world.

Physical violence and emotional abuse, such as demeaning comments, are unacceptable, no matter the excuse. There is no defense for these sorts of actions, and, if they are occurring, professional help is needed immediately, without exception.

Please read this carefully:

If this is occurring, there is nothing in this book, or any other, that can help you. Get professional help. Whether you're on the receiving end of this action or the one doling it out, get professional help.

On the other hand, working through normal struggles in a healthy manner actually has the potential to strengthen your bond. People who go through hardships together usually end up much closer in the end.

Consider military buddies who have gone to war together, or mountain climbers who have summited a high peak, or a couple who has been married for 40 years and seen it all, good and bad — together. All of these teams have a certain bond that can't be broken, and that unbreakable bond wouldn't exist if they hadn't worked through adversity together.

The fact is, if you want your marriage to last, you're going to have to work on it.

We've all heard that, but exactly what does that mean? That's where we come to the Action Plan.

The Action Plan is a step-by-step checklist of specific daily actions you'll take to maintain a happy, healthy relationship.

This exercise is very important for the "about to be married," the "newly married," and even the "we've been happily married for years and want to stay that way." In fact, it's great for anyone who is in a relationship at all.

I highly recommend you work together on this as a couple—it's tremendously powerful. It will help you identify those things that are most important to you—and your partner. Otherwise, you may include items on your Action Plan that aren't actually important to your partner.

Even worse, you may not include things that are actually extremely important to your partner that you weren't even aware of! Only by having open, honest, positive discussion can you truly find out.

The communications aspect of going through this exercise together may end up being one of the most important things you do as a married couple, as it compels you to discuss issues that can help build a close, loving relationship, or tear one down if not addressed.

Discussing ways to keep each other happy early on can save a lot of pain in the future. Remember, the smallest pebble in your shoe can feel like a boulder if you have walked on it for too long.

If it's already reached the 'boulder stage', that's okay, too. Now is the time to identify it, and work on getting rid of it once and for all.

If, for whatever reason, you are unable to work on this together, you can certainly begin by doing it yourself. Your spouse may see your own commitment, and follow suit later on. Either way, you're doing your best, and that's all you have control of.

Exercise: Pull out a blank sheet of paper. Write down the following questions and your answers to them:

How would you rate your relationship on a scale of 1–10?

How do you think your partner would rate it?

What are some areas of your relationship you feel particularly good about?

What are some areas you feel could use some work?

DEVELOPING YOUR "OXCART"

Now it's time to develop your Success and Failure Scenarios, and your Action Plan. As we discussed before, the way in which you develop these plans is absolutely crucial. You have to develop your scenarios with all of the detail and emotion you can muster.

Remember, we act on emotion every single day. It's that emotion that drives us to success or failure, and it's that emotion, that passion, that you will harness to inspire you to take the actions that ensure success.

I come from an interesting perspective on this. I've been divorced. I know what it feels like to have a failed marriage, and it is a terrible, terrible feeling. If you've been there, you know exactly what I'm talking about. I'm remarried, and I'm going to do everything in my power to make sure this marriage truly is "'til death do us part."

That passion drives me to work on my marriage, every single day. I may not have complete control over both sides of it, but I have complete control over my side of it, and that's the side I take complete responsibility for.

THE SUCCESS SCENARIO

As I mentioned, the first part of developing your Oxcart Technique is writing your Success Scenario. In doing so, if you simply write, "Have a happy marriage" on the Success Scenario, and "Divorce" on the Failure Scenario, that will cut down your success rate immensely.

Again, emotion is the driver of all action. Effective Scenarios will have detail and emotion throughout. They will move you emotionally, and make you want to take action, or avoid certain actions.

Before reading further, please take a moment to visualize a couple of things. First of all, what are the things you love most about your spouse?

Remember back to some of the great times you two have had together. What are the three times you've had the most fun you've ever had together? Play each occasion in your mind.

In producing your Success Scenario, regardless of the topic, it works best if you take the time to visualize what achieving that goal would look like.

Now that you're feeling all warm and fuzzy (hopefully!), let's start making your Success Scenario.

This works best if you start by making a list. After you've listed all the points, it's easier to write out your Success Scenario in paragraph form. For instance, what would your dream marriage look like? What things would you do together? How would it feel?

Please take out a piece of paper, or your computer, if you prefer, and start listing these points. Remember, this book is all about you actually breaking through the barriers, not just reading about it!

Here's an example of an actual Success Scenario for a happy marriage:

> Deb and I are deeply in love. When I look in her eyes, I feel that excitement in the pit of my stomach that I felt when I first realized I loved her. When we kiss, she still literally takes my breath away. We hold hands even when we're just sitting together on the couch, or walking into the store.
>
> We do new, active things together, and truly enjoy each other's company. We camp, play games, see movies, go to museums, travel, and see new places together, and learn about their history. We can still talk for hours about nothing and everything.
>
> I respect her and adore her, and I can tell by the look in her eyes, and her smile, and her gentle touch, that she feels the same way about me. We sup-

port each other in our goals, and help each other accomplish them, to the extent that we're asked to. We give each other the space we need to thrive on our own, as well. We share the workload so neither of us feels taken advantage of.

We regularly do things for each other out of love and kindness, with no regard to payback. We respect each other's opinions, even if they're different than our own. We talk over challenges and disagreements with a nurturing attitude. We stay fit to remain physically attractive to each other, and to maintain good health into the future. We're intimate with tenderness, caring, and excitement.

We make time for each other every single day. We have fun, and we laugh, and we giggle, and make stupid jokes, and act goofy. I'm there for her when she needs me, and she's there for me when I need her. We're proud of each other, for the person we are. We're by each other's side and support each other completely. We're an unbreakable team. I love her with all of my heart.

THIS IS MY FUTURE. I WILL DO WHATEVER IT TAKES TO MAKE THIS HAPPEN. TODAY, I WILL TAKE THE ACTIONS IN MY PLAN SO I MAY ENJOY THE HAPPINESS I DESERVE.

What a beautiful Success Scenario! That seems to me to be a scenario that would help keep us all on track. Unfortunately, for most of the marriages, it's simply not enough. Again, understanding that Prospect Theory taught us we'll do more to avoid pain than go toward pleasure, it's critical that we build that 'stick' into the equation to keep us doing the things we should be doing every single day, and make sure we don't do the things we shouldn't.

THE FAILURE SCENARIO

Now it's time for the "stick" part of the technique — the Failure Scenario. This part won't be so fun. By the time you have written this part, your subconscious should be screaming, "There is no way in the world I'm going to let that happen!"

Stop reading for a moment, and take the time to visualize this as well:

What's the worst-case scenario if your marriage falls apart? How bad will it feel? What things will be different? How will it affect the rest of your life? Who else will be affected by it? Are there children involved? How will it affect their lives?

Again, please stop reading and go through this exercise. It's important.

That feels terrible, doesn't it? It's worth taking action every single day to make sure it never happens, isn't it? That's the power of the Failure Scenario.

Read the following Failure Scenario, and see if this would create enough emotion in someone to get them to stick to their plan:

> Our marriage has failed, and Deb is filing for divorce. The dreams we once had together are gone. I feel dead inside. I may never see my sons (stepsons) again. All the love that we felt, the closeness as a family, is gone.
>
> My house, once filled with laughter and arguing, and fun, and singing, and yelling, and love, is completely quiet now. All I can hear are sounds of the house settling, and of my grandfather clock ticking time away. The items my kids gave me in love just make me hugely sad when I look at them.
>
> I've now failed in my second marriage, and I'm not sure I'll want to ever try for a third. At this point, a bit past my prime, I may end up not having someone to go into old age with; certainly no one whom I've had years of memories with, years of challenges, and joys, and tears, and building a relationship that only comes through the passage of time. No one who loves me deeply to be there for me, as I'm needing her in my old age, and no one to be there for.
>
> My years will be lonely now. No wife, no kids, no grandkids. No one to visit my grave, or remember my name for generations. Worst of all, through action or inaction, I've hurt the person I love most in this world. The love I used to see in her eyes is replaced by emptiness and contempt. I know she's hurting as bad as I am. Maybe worse. I'll never feel her loving touch again.
>
> We'll never share coffee and talk for hours. We won't travel together, or be together, or even want to be in the same room together again. The team

that was supposed to be "her and me against the world" is now divided, and fighting against itself. My love is lost. My hope is lost. I am lost.

MY FUTURE WILL BE DIFFERENT. I HAVE THE POWER TO ENSURE MY SUCCESS SCENARIO BECOMES MY NEW REALITY. I WILL DO THE FOLLOWING TO MAKE SURE I SUCCEED IN REACHING MY GOAL.

I can tell you that just reading that one makes me personally feel very deep emotions! I would do whatever it took to avoid a Failure Scenario like that, and I'm sure the person who wrote it feels the same way!

ACTION PLAN

Now we come to the bottom-line information: the actual Plan itself. These steps are what will mean the difference between a happy and a failed marriage.

How do you find out what things will make and keep your spouse happy? What things will make them want to be with you and stay with you for the long run?

This is where it gets technical. Get ready for this. Are you ready? Okay, here it is:

ASK THEM!

That's right — communicate!

That one little word makes all the difference, but most of us do far too little of it.

Talk with your loved one about what their expectations and desires are for the different areas of your relationship. Find out what makes them happy, or unhappy, as the case may be.

For ideas on what to discuss, let's get input from someone who has been involved with the failed side of many marriages: Leisa Toomey, a divorce attorney in Sunshine Coast, Australia. In an article she wrote on July 7, 2013, she explained that the top 10 reasons for divorce are:

- Infidelity
- Communication Breakdown

- Physical, Psychological, or Emotional Abuse
- Financial Issues
- Sexual Incompatibility
- Boredom
- Religious and Cultural Strains
- Child Rearing
- Addiction
- Differences in Priorities and Expectations

This list provides a perfect starting point for your discussion.

How are you going to keep the lines of communication open?

What are financial concerns each of you has, and how are you going to work through them?

What priorities do you both have in life? How can you support each other in accomplishing those?

What are your thoughts on raising your children, and who has what responsibilities?

You can go through each of the points above, along with others you may think of, and write down notes—it's that important.

Then formulate all of this into an Action Plan that you can follow to the best of your abilities, each and every day.

If the discussion gets a little heated, that's perfect! That means you have identified places where you need to communicate even more. NOT talking about them would only have caused misunderstandings and disappointments down the road.

The following is an actual Action Plan, to give you one example of what it can look like.

Again, whatever you do, don't just copy my plan as your own. I included it to give you an example of what each of the sections CAN look like, not what they SHOULD look like. What they SHOULD look like is completely up to you.

You'll need to develop a completely unique plan, depending on the wants for both of you, the needs and the desires, as well as your own unique personalities. It has to feel like your own, with your own emotion and personal conviction. It won't be nearly as effective unless it comes from your heart.

Happy Marriage Action Plan:

I will always be faithful to Deb, in every way. I won't put myself in situations that might be compromising. I won't flirt with other women, in person, online, or otherwise. I will keep away from pornography, and will do my best to watch my eyes in public.

I will continue to keep the lines of communication open with Deb. When something is bothering me, I'll bring it up to her in a private, respectful manner, focusing on solving the problem, without assessing blame.

I will always be loving, nurturing, caring, and supportive in my relationship with Deb, both verbally and non-verbally. I want what's best for her, and my words and actions will reflect that, always.

My love life with Deb will continue to be tender and exciting. I will continue to take care of myself physically. I will strive to create a romantic atmosphere and show her how much I care, at all times.

I will tell her several times a day that I love her. I will hold her hand and hug her, and kiss her for no apparent reason whatsoever. I'll do nice things for her, often, with no expectation of return. I will surprise her with flowers, notes, cards, and little gifts when it's completely unexpected.

I will look for new and fun ways to spend time with Deb. We will continue to have adventures together, making sure we don't get stuck in a rut of just getting through life and taking care of the family. We'll build our own memories together where we get out and have fun, experiencing new things together.

I'll continue to give Deb the space she needs to be her own person and live her own life.

I will respect Deb's views, especially when they're different from my own. I will remember that one of the many reasons I love her is that she's a strong, independent woman, able to stand on her own two feet and have her own opinion. We'll continue to have conversations about our opposing viewpoints from the standpoint of learning from each other, being open to potentially adopting each other's views instead of just arguing for our own. Instead of being an argument to win, it is a conversation that's won by learning to appreciate each other even more. We can also agree to disagree on topics, and still respect each other as a person—in fact, even more so because of our differences.

I'll be a gentleman with her at all times in all ways. I'll continue to open doors for her and help her with her coat. And I'll keep my bodily noises to myself.

I will help with cooking meals, washing dishes, and helping out around the house, along with my personal chores.

Deb and I will continue to talk nearly every night about our direction with the boys, how we're raising them — triumphs, challenges, concerns, and solutions.

We will also discuss our goals as a family, as a couple, and as individuals. We'll discuss each of our parts in those goals, whether we're meeting each other's expectations, and helping each other.

I will love her with all my heart.

Again, it's tremendously powerful to do this exercise as a couple. It's particularly healthy to talk together about what the ultimate relationship would look like, from each other's standpoint. It's also powerful to talk about the emotional aspect of breaking up, and to share each other's sorrow. You can work on the Action Plan together, discussing each of the points together as you write them out, or you can do this exercise separately and come together and compare what you've each written. Either way you do it will provide a perfect opportunity to have some open, frank communication about what is important to both of you. In this way, your Action Plan becomes a potent communication tool, as well.

As the immortal Zig Ziglar said,

"Many marriages would be better if the husband and the
wife clearly understood that they are on the same side."

One of the sights that brings the most warmth to my heart is when I see an elderly couple obviously in love. I love the way they look at each other. You can feel the connection between them, with understanding that only years of challenges, and good times, and sadness, and joys, and disappointments, and adventures together can bring. I love watching them walking together, still holding hands after all these years. I truly hope the information here, along with your own hard work, dedication, and caring, enables your relationship to be a rewarding one for the rest of your days together.

Always remember the words of the popular author and journalist, Mignon Mc-Laughlin:

"A successful marriage requires falling in love
many times, always with the same person."

It takes work. But I don't think there's anything more worthwhile in the whole world.

SELF-EXAMINATION QUESTION: What are the top 3 most important reasons your relationship is important to you? Is it worth doing what it takes to work on it every single day?

CHAPTER 21

Healing Personal Relationships

*A life filled with love must have some thorns, but
a life empty of love will have no roses.*

— Unknown

Our relationships may be the single most important factor in our lives. If things are going well with the people we're around most, our day is filled with joy. Even if we have challenges and setbacks in our lives, the people we are close to can lift us up and help us conquer, or at least be there for us as we cry on their shoulder.

On the other hand, if we are having relationship difficulties with someone around us, it can darken our entire outlook. It can even put us in a bad enough mood that we snap at others, and make us less effective with our jobs, our families, and everything else we're around.

Exercise: Think about someone close to you that you've had some relationship challenges with. Before you read on, please take a moment to visualize the two of you having an argument.

219

How do you feel right now? If you did the exercise, you probably feel pretty lousy.

Exercise: Now, take a moment and think about someone close to you that you're getting along well with.

Now, how do you feel? Probably pretty good.

As you can see, our relationships affect us in ways we sometimes don't even see. We may not even realize it, but those around us probably do.

It's not easy to work on relationships. In fact, it can be very hard, as facing up to any challenge can be at times. It's certainly emotional, and it can take a lot out of us. On the other hand, ignoring the problem is harder over the long run and a lot more costly.

Exercise: As you read the following list of people you have relationships with, please consider what that relationship is like: good, bad, or somewhere in between. Then write down on a separate sheet of paper any with whom you might be having challenges.

- Boss
- Coworker
- Subordinate
- Parent
- Sister or brother
- Son or daughter
- Step-family member
- Mother- or father-in-law
- Other relative
- Friend
- Ex-wife or ex-husband
- Girlfriend or boyfriend
- Teacher or someone else at school
- Someone in an organization you're part of
- Anyone you're around on an ongoing basis

Are there any of those people whom you feel you would like to have a better relationship with?

Again, this book isn't meant to replace expert knowledge on relationships. These experts spend years studying and practicing to provide a service to those who need them. I highly recommend taking advantage of their dedication and expertise. What I want to do is to help provide the framework to fit that knowledge into, and to build in the motivation that will help you actually heed that advice long term, to make a difference in your life. I want to teach you how to apply The Oxcart Technique to virtually any goal, to greatly increase your chances of achieving it. In this case, I want you to have better relationships.

This is an important chapter, and it may be the hardest category to work on. In a marriage, there are two people who (hopefully) want very badly to work on the relationship and make it the best it can be. In our relationships outside of that, both parties may not be motivated to reconcile. You're obviously already having challenges in this relationship, and may not even be on speaking terms.

Chances are, there's mistrust involved. Even your intentions might be questioned. It's most likely going to involve breaking through some walls to begin with, and this may not be possible in all cases. If the other person is not agreeable to working on improving your relationship, it's going to make it a lot harder.

That doesn't mean improving your relationship is impossible. You can still do everything possible by yourself to improve the relationship, and hope that it's enough to make them want to do the same in the future. Either way, you can rest easy knowing that you've done what you can, and that's all you can ask of yourself.

To attempt to engage them, you might start the conversation with something to the effect of, "Our relationship is very important to me, and I care about you" (if you honestly do!). "I feel we could have an even stronger relationship, and I was wondering if you would do me a favor. I recently read a book that showed me a very powerful method for working things out, and I'd like to give it a try with you. Would you do that for me?"

Naturally, those are my words. You'll want to put everything in your very own words, in a way that might be effective with the individual.

The next step will be to establish your Failure Scenario. Who or what will be hurt if your relationship doesn't improve? Do you both care about that person or thing? If so, that would be very healthy to discuss, as it has the potential to bring you both on the same side, coming up with a solution that would keep you from hurting the person you both care about. That takes the emphasis off of you and puts it on a positive note of helping those people or projects you care about.

For example, "If we keep on locking horns, it's only going to hurt Jamie. But if we're able to get through our differences, I know there will be less stress when we're all together! Wouldn't that be nice?" Or "Our differences are hurting both the morale and the productivity of our office. Imagine how much more powerful we would be if you and I were able to work together better."

Let's start with an example that many people can relate to: bad feelings between siblings.

Stephanie and her brother, Roger, are both good people; they're just both very opinionated, as siblings can tend to be. We won't go into everything that happened to get them to this point—all too often, digging into the garbage only brings up things that stink. It can open old wounds and bring the focus back to the negative past, instead of the positive future.

The result of their years of fighting is that they both refuse to be in the same house together, and they haven't talked in years. Holidays have gone by, as have the years, and memories go with them. The death of their father and the arguments that ensued only widened the chasm and deepened the misgivings.

As usual when people are fighting, it's those around them that suffer the most. Their mother hasn't had a holiday with the whole family in almost a decade. Their children have never met their aunt or uncle, and the only things they've heard about them are negative. They have cousins they'll never get to know and a family support system that won't be there when times are tough.

It was Roger's wife, Betty, who showed them The Oxcart Technique and who first wrote out a Failure Scenario for them, so they could see the damage their arguing was doing to those around them. It was that, and only that, which finally got their attention.

> "I guess I was just too busy being mad to see how it was really affecting my mom, Betty, and the boys," admitted Roger. "I realized how selfish I was being, and I guess how stubborn, too. This is my sister, after all. She may pi** me off to no end, but she's still my sister. If we're ever going to be a family again, I guess we'd better start now. So I'm going to try to swallow my pride, get over myself, and make a go of it. Not so much for myself, but for my mom, for Betty, and for my kids."

What finally got Roger's attention after all of these years? Here's the Failure Scenario Betty wrote for them:

> "It's our first Christmas without mom. Her one and only Christmas wish never came to be: to have her son and daughter actually together on that night that meant so much to her, sharing the love the family used to enjoy when everyone was younger, and less angry with the world and those they once loved. Her last tears ran down her face in her hospital room; she knew that when she passed, her children wouldn't all be with her, because they were both too stubborn to leave the past where it belongs and put out the effort that it takes sometimes to keep relationships going.
>
> She feels that she failed as a mother—she's mentioned that many times— because she couldn't raise a family that had love—only hate. Our children don't know their own cousins, or even their aunt and uncle. If something happens to us, they won't have any family to turn to, only friends or strang-

ers. Even worse: Our example to them is that hate is stronger than love. Family isn't as important as pride. Grudges are meant to be held strongly. The past controls the future. Our example may cause them to act the same way when they're older.

We may have the same problems with them on holidays, or on our own deathbeds. Perhaps we'll even have the chasms between them and us, where hearts are turned cold and resentments are given more power than forgiveness."

What a terrible feeling! Roger actually came to tears when he read this, and realized the impact that his ongoing arguments were having on those he loved. The bottom line was: He loved his mother more than he hated his sister. And the truth is, he really did love his sister. He had just let the wound fester much longer than he should have, and it was making his heart sick. Looking at the worst possible scenario—one that could very much become a reality— was the kick in the butt he needed to take action.

The next step you will take in working on your own relationship will be building the Success Scenario together—what you'd like your relationship to look like. If it's a job- or business-related relationship, how much better will the project, or business, be overall, if the two of you are able to improve your interactions? How many other people will be impacted?

If it's a relationship in an organization, such as a charity you're both involved in, is the cause of the organization important enough to both of you to get along? What would that look like, and what impact would it have on the organization and those it affects? If it's a family relationship, why is it important that you are, at the very least, amicable? What's the best-case scenario, and how does that feel?

Roger felt an amazing sense of relief as he was writing his Success Scenario. It was as if the weight of the world was lifting off of his shoulders. He approached his sister Stephanie very carefully, and found her more receptive than he expected.

Maybe she wasn't such a bad person, after all. He shared what he had written with her, and they agreed to work together on refining it, to make sure it contained elements that were important to both of them—the first positive thing they'd agreed on in years.

I found what they wrote quite beautiful:

> It's Christmas morning, and we're all together at Mom's house for the first time in years. She is absolutely beaming—the happiest we've seen her for as long as we can remember! That huge smile as she watches all of her grandchildren opening presents and squealing with delight warms our hearts to the core. The sounds of laughter and joy ring through the house that is usually so quiet.
>
> All of the children run off and play together, while the five of us sit around the Christmas tree and open the presents we've given to each other, and we talk about the old times before all the fighting began. We still disagree on many issues, but we respect each other's views and don't try to convince each other to believe the way we believe.
>
> We get together as a family a few times a year as our schedules allow, and build back the trust and love we once shared. We're there for each other in the hard times, and we can always depend on each other for moral support and a kind word when we're down.
>
> God willing, when Mom passes, she'll do so with the feeling of having her entire family around her, praying together, sending her to heaven with a heart full of love and her soul rejoicing, knowing she accomplished the most important thing in her life: raising a loving family.
>
> We set an example for our children that sins are meant to be forgiven, that yesterday's baggage should be left behind, and that love endures over all.
>
> Finally, we're a family again!
>
> THIS IS MY FUTURE. I WILL DO WHATEVER IT TAKES TO MAKE THIS HAPPEN. TODAY, I WILL TAKE THE ACTIONS IN MY PLAN SO I MAY ENJOY THE HAPPINESS I DESERVE.

Both of them, along with their spouses, are committed to doing whatever it takes to make sure their future is the Success Scenario and not the Failure

Scenario, even if it means biting their tongues and taking a "time out" upon occasion. Again, a major power of The Oxcart Technique is experiencing the feelings of both the possibility of success and of failure, and the effects it will have on both of you, and on people or things that are important to you.

What are those steps that will make the difference between your own relationship success or failure? Again, it brings us right back to the Action Plan.

YOUR ACTION PLAN

Just as in the Happy Marriage Action Plan, it's possible to write the Relationship Action Plan by yourself, but it's not recommended. The absence of communication between the two of you could cause unintentional misunderstandings and, therefore, misgivings.

How so? It's easy to write down actions that should be taken from your point of view. It may be a little more difficult trying to see it from the other person's point of view as well, but it's critical that you do.

If you merely write actions you'd like the other person to take to make things right, you've only written down half the dance steps. As my mom used to say when I'd blame my brother for an argument, "It takes two to Tango." Do your best to see the dispute from the other person's point of view.

You may even talk to other people who are involved and ask them to recommend actions for you to take to make amends and move forward. It's amazing how people can open up when you prove to them that you're willing to take actions to make things better.

If you're working on the Action Plan together, you may find this to be either a healing or a contentious process, depending on the attitudes of both parties going in. If the goal is to point fingers, determine fault, and make the other party pay for their wrongdoings, there will be no joy in Mudville.

If, on the other hand, both parties can focus on actions that can be taken by everyone to avoid the Failure Scenario and see the Success Scenario to completion, the act of working together on action points can be therapeutic, and potentially even heal some wounds.

If things do get a little heated, it may be necessary to take several "time outs" during this process, and perhaps even use a disinterested third party intermediary, such as a counselor. It's important not to focus on blame, or why things got the way they are, but rather on what actions can be taken to mend relations going forward.

As long as the pleasure of the carrot and the pain of the stick are stronger emotions than the negative feelings that have built up between you, you should be able to stay focused.

Some questions to consider are:

What actions should be avoided in the future?

What actions should be taken that haven't been in the past?

What can be done to work better together in the future?

Remember, a great relationship is about two things: first, appreciating the similarities, and second, respecting the differences.

As one example, here's Roger's Action Plan for his relationship with Stephanie. It may not be perfect, but it's a great starting point. Then again, it's not about perfection; it's about taking positive steps toward the Success Scenario and away from the Failure Scenario.

Even with all of this in place, it won't be easy. It would be easy to fall back into the same old habits and let the old feelings bubble back to the surface. Only the pain of the stick and the pleasure of the carrot will give Roger the power he needs to take the actions he so wants to take.

Roger's Action Plan

- I will respect Stephanie's political beliefs, religious beliefs, and personal beliefs. Whether I agree with them or not, she is free to believe them, and I won't try to convince her to believe as I do. We agree to disagree, and to not worry about it.

- I won't bring up my political, religious, or personal beliefs that conflict with Stephanie's. We'll avoid any topics that might cause a confrontation. There are many more things we can talk about.
- If Stephanie brings up sensitive topics, I will respectfully ask her to change the subject. I will happily change the subject if she asks me to do the same.
- I will do my best to make only supportive statements to her, and not correct her when I think she's wrong.
- For the time being, I won't drink more than one drink when I'm around her, to help keep my attitude in check.
- I will make only kind comments about her in front of other people, most especially the kids.
- I will look for the good in Stephanie, and focus on the fact that:

  - She is a loving, caring mother.
  - She is a faithful wife to Toby.
  - She is a bright, independent thinker.
  - She has a great sense of humor.
  - She always looks on the bright side.
  - She is a very hard worker.
  - She volunteers her time at the school, and for other causes that are important to her.

- For the good of our family, and for myself, I will work hard every day to put the past in the past, and build a positive relationship with my sister.

Exercise: Do me a favor, and go back to the list of people in your life that you wrote on the piece of paper at the beginning of this chapter. Identify one of them that you are having difficulties with. Take the time after you've read this paragraph to write out a Success Scenario for your relationship with them.

What would it look like if your relationship would greatly improve? Who are all the people that would benefit? How would times together improve? How would the other people involved have their lives changed? How would that feel?

Visualize for a moment what it looks like if the relationship doesn't improve. In fact, what if it gets worse? Let's go all the way: What's the worst-case scenario? Who are all the people that this will hurt?

Now, go back and read both of these scenarios.

Pretty powerful, isn't it?

I realize it won't be easy going through this exercise. All too often we try to avoid dealing with our troubled relationships, because they are painful to face. Unfortunately, the problem won't go away by itself. It usually just gets worse and worse, as bad feelings build upon bad feelings.

So the million dollar question is this: Is going through the pain of working together with them on this exercise worth the pleasure it will bring to those you care about? Will either avoiding the terrible Failure Scenario you described, or seeing that situation improve as you've written in your Success Scenario, provide strong enough motivation to get you to take action? If so, then with courage on your first step, it's time to get to work.

SELF-EXAMINATION QUESTION: Who do you need to improve your relationship with? Who all does it affect if you don't do this? Why is that important to you?

CHAPTER 22

The Grand Finale

The successful warrior is the average man, with laser-like focus.

— Bruce Lee

You have now learned a tremendously powerful technique to achieve any goal. You have learned very specific applications for that technique, such as:

- building a retirement fund,
- healing relationships,
- building businesses and organizations,
- inspiring your team,
- managing your weight, and
- overcoming an addiction.

However, whatever you do, don't limit yourself to applying this technique to only these areas!

You can use The Oxcart Technique for any goal you can think of, no matter how large or small!

Do you want to inspire yourself and your team to greater success? Develop an Oxcart! Lose a few pounds and keep it off for good? Develop an Oxcart! Want to actually double the size of your business, help a relationship, do well in sports, become a famous actor, get out of debt, do well in school, or just buy a boat — the possibilities are truly endless!

The point is, to reach any goal, you need an Action Plan, and the motivation to stick to it.

You've gained the knowledge. Now the question is, what are you going to do with it? Are you going to say, "That was a good book. I'll have to do that some-time" and put it away, without taking any new action?

It sounds sad, but many people do exactly that! Perhaps you have before. I know I have!

Or are you going to set up your Scenarios and Action Plan, but decide you don't want to post them anywhere because that would seem goofy, and have them get lost in the shuffle?

Maybe you'll build them, post them, and perhaps even read them for several days, until you forget, or other things get in the way. Then the passion fades over time, and you find yourself exactly where you were before.

Even this book and the knowledge in it isn't a "magic pill." Your life isn't going to change because you read it.

Your life will change because you implement it. The "work" part of this WORK-book doesn't stop here—it's just beginning!

If you want long-term results, you have to take long-term action.

You have to continue working with and modifying your plans, as both you and your circumstances change. You have to make your Oxcart a living, breathing part of you—your companion along your journey that helps keep you on task.

Your quest isn't complete until the day you die — and I'm not even sure it's complete then!

The great news is, you have a precise method to develop the road map, the inspiration, and the passion, to help guide you and give you strength along the way.

Will you use it?

I pray that you're one of the people I've been thinking about as I wrote this book: someone who will latch onto this knowledge and apply it to its fullest.

Someone who will identify one or more goals that they want to accomplish, and stick to their Action Plan until they've achieved success in that area.

Someone whose life is made better in some way because they read this book, and acted on it.

If you are, please let me know on my website: www.TerryLFossum.com.

Before we come to the end of this book, I'll leave you with one last story:

Late in the spring of 2012, I decided it was time to take a road trip, so I pulled out my maps to see where the road might take me.

'Hmmm…' I thought to myself.

"The Arctic Circle. That looks cool! I think I'll do it!"

After an 'interesting' conversation with my wife and a little work on my Chevy Blazer, I took off on a 6,000 mile solo driving, boating, and backpacking adventure of a lifetime.

In Inuvik, in the Northwest Territories of Canada, I met an Inuvialuit guide by the name of Kylik, who arranged for a boat to drop me off out on the permafrost, deep in the Mackenzie Delta. Accompanied only by literally millions of mosquitos and whatever other creatures came my way, I backpacked, camped, and enjoyed the amazing sights and solitude.

When I returned to Inuvik via Tuktoyaktuk, Kylik asked if I wanted to join him and some friends on a caribou hunt. The answer was a very quick "Absolutely!" I'm not a hunter myself, but I respect that they hunt so they can eat; and I wasn't about to pass up an opportunity like that. Can you imagine? Hunting Caribou with the Inuits deep in the Arctic Circle — What a crazy, great opportunity!

Enjoying 24 hours a day of sunlight, we hunted literally all night long until we came across the great herd at about 6 o'clock in the morning. It was an amazing sight: Hundreds and hundreds of caribou stretched across the frozen tundra, as far as the eye could see. The hunters were fortunate enough to get six of them, plenty to restock their stores that had been depleted over the long, dark, and frozen arctic winter. We spent the next 6 hours hauling meat back to their truck. Needless to say, I was completely exhausted; even simply walking had become difficult for me.

They asked me to go back to Inuvik with them, one of them offering the great honor of joining his family at their whaling village, a distinction usually offered only to close family. It sounded incredible, but something deep in my gut was telling me to go south to Dawson in the Yukon.

Add to this that a serious arctic storm had developed, blasting freezing cold winds all around us. My Inuvialuit friends urged me to go back north with them to Inuvik, since traveling by myself could be very dangerous right now. But something kept telling me that I had to go south.

The final nail in the coffin: I was out of gas. The driver of the other truck mistakenly poured all of the gas in the Gerry can into his tank. There wasn't a gas station for miles and miles and miles. And there wasn't anything AT ALL for miles and miles and miles.

There was no way in the world I could make it on a nearly empty tank. Now everything that made sense screamed out that I had to go back north to Inuvik with them — everything, except for that feeling in my gut that said I had to go south.

Covered in blood from the hunt and completely exhausted, I began my perilous journey south. When I would begin to fall asleep at the wheel, I would pull over to the side of the "road" and pass out for about 5 minutes, and then begin again.

I couldn't do this too often, as shutting off and starting the engine wasted precious drops of fuel. Any time I made it to the top of a hill, I would take the engine out of gear and coast to the bottom.

And something seemingly miraculous happened: Those blasting winds became a tail wind, pushing me along from behind. I made many, many extra miles virtually on wind power alone. With a low fuel warning light that had been on for a very long time, non-stop prayer, and the last fumes in my tank, I pulled into the remote gas station that was my saving grace.

I made camp at a trickling stream outside of Dawson and stripped off my blood-soaked clothes, including my one and only coat — a duster that had gone on countless adventures with me. I placed all of them in the stream to wash off some of the blood, with large rocks on them "just in case."

When I awoke a few hours later, the trickling stream had been replaced by a raging river! My clothes! My gun belt! MY COAT! There was no way they could still be at the bottom of that raging river! I considered my options, questioned my sanity, stripped down again, and began wading into the frigid waters.

Amazingly, my clothes were still down there! After getting them to the top through the ripping current, I laid them out to dry, and went to try to find someone who could explain the phenomenon of the sudden river.

"You haven't heard?" the local explained. "There's a terrible storm up north. It washed out everything! The road, the ferry — it's all gone!"

The road I had just come down was no more. If I had waited, there's no telling what might have happened to me.

There will be times when people will tell you that you can't accomplish your goals. They may even truly have your best interests in mind. There will be distractions that will try to strip your focus from your goal.

Every excuse in the world may come up, even valid ones, and try to convince you it can't be done. You may be far past exhaustion and have all of the odds stacked against you; but you must go on.

You must listen to that feeling in your gut that says you must go on. No matter the obstacles, no matter the circumstances, no matter the possibilities or the impossibilities, you must go on.

ALL IN, OR NOTHING AT ALL!

Then, and only then, can you experience the true elation that comes from hard work and perseverance, and achieving something that means the world to you.

It's an exciting time of promise and possibilities. And you have the power in your hands.

~

Thank you for being here with me on our journey, and I wish you the best of joy and success as you take your next steps on your own.

I'll leave you with the same words I told my boys when they left to school each morning:

MAKE THE WORLD A BETTER PLACE...BECAUSE YOU'RE IN IT!

EXERCISE: Immediately schedule on your calendar to tune up your Oxcart Technique every week for 1 month, then every month for the first year. It's that important.

FINAL WORD FROM THE AUTHOR:
What difference has this book made in your life?

Has this book made a difference in your life? I'd love to hear from you! Drop by www.TerryLFossum.com or scan the QR code below and let me know!

Would you like me to personally coach you using the Oxcart Technique to excel in all aspects of your life: Your business or career, your relationships, your health, or any other goal? Let's connect and see if we're a good fit!

Are you interested in having me give an energetic talk to your company or organization that not only fires them up, but helps them greatly increase performance and be happier in their lives as well?

Find out more at www.TerryLFossum.com, or at the QR code below.

There you'll also gain access to loads of free content, inspiration, updates, and so much more.

And finally, If you would give me the honor of recommending this book to your friends, family, and coworkers in person and on social media, I would be extremely grateful. It is my hope that this information will literally help people around the globe reach their goals, hopes, and dreams that they may never have reached otherwise.

At this point in my life, it's all about making the world a better place. And I truly believe that, working together, we really can make that happen. Thank you for being part of that!

Keep Up the Good Fight,

—Terry

www.TerryLFossum.com

ABOUT THE AUTHOR

Terry L. Fossum grew up in the poorest city in the entire United States of America, McAllen, TX on the border of Mexico, surrounded by gangs and drugs. When he was in middle school, he found himself staring down the barrel of an assault rifle in his own back alley, wondering if his next breath would be his last. In high school, his father was killed. Before he died, one of the neighbors came up to him and said, "I just want to make sure you understand something: Not a single one of your sons will ever grow up to be anything."

That's not the way it turned out.

As a Captain in the United States Air Force, Terry was the Executive Officer for an entire Group of nuclear B-52 bombers during the Cold War. He was honored as the Fairchild Air Force Base Officer of the Year, Humanitarian of the Year for all of Strategic Air Command, and Distinguished Graduate from Squadron Officer's School.

Terry is a highly successful international businessman, building, training, and inspiring sales teams around the globe, reaching the top fraction of 1% of his industry in the world.

As an Eagle Scout and Scoutmaster, he represented the Boy Scouts of America on a television survival reality show and won.

He is a TV Host, Actor, Producer, and Voiceover artist, winning Best Supporting Actor and Fan Favorite at the 2021 Christian Film Festival.

He is the #1 Bestselling Author on The Wall Street Journal, Amazon, and Barnes & Noble, and Bestselling Author on USAToday.

His TEDxTalk debuted at #2 in the world, and has been called 'One of the most impactful TEDxTalks of this century'.

He serves on numerous boards and has philanthropic projects in different parts of the world.

In addition to being a Black Belt in Tae Kwon Do, Terry is a global adventurer including solo backpacking deep into the Arctic Circle, survival in the Amazon Jungle, and a trek deep into the mountains of Rwanda searching for elusive Silverback Gorillas. He has been named Los Angeles Magazine's 2024 Person of the Year, and Insights Success Magazine has named him 'The Most Impactful and Visionary Personality to Look for in 2025'.

Terry is considered a world-class keynote speaker, a human potential expert and success coach, and considers himself a smitten husband and a proud dad of three amazing stepsons.

"Never let anyone or any circumstance decide your future. You and you alone have complete control over it. Take control now, and never let go."

— **Terry L. Fossum**